Proficiency in
GRAMMAR
and
LANGUAGE
for CSEC®

T0355332

L. A. Forde   L. G. Marsh

OXFORD
UNIVERSITY PRESS

OXFORD
UNIVERSITY PRESS

Great Clarendon Street, Oxford, OX2 6DP, United Kingdom

Oxford University Press is a department of the University of Oxford.
It furthers the University's objective of excellence in research, scholarship,
and education by publishing worldwide. Oxford is a registered trade mark of
Oxford University Press in the UK and in certain other countries

First published by Hulton Educational Publications Ltd in 1985
Second edition published by Nelson Thornes Ltd
This edition published by Oxford University Press in 2014

British Library Cataloguing in Publication Data
Data available

978-0-7175-1370-3

37

Printed in the UK by Ashford Colour Ltd

The manufacturer's authorised representative in the EU for
product safety is Oxford University Press España S.A. of El Parque
Empresarial San Fernando de Henares, Avenida de Castilla, 2 –
28830 Madrid (www.oup.es/en or product.safety@oup.com).
OUP España S.A. also acts as importer into Spain of products
made by the manufacturer.

BEFORE YOU BEGIN

TO THE STUDENT

The syllabus of the Caribbean Secondary Education Certificate describes one of its objectives as 'a practical concern for precision, clarity and grammatical correctness in the use of language.' Before you begin to work through the lessons in this book, think for a moment about language. How can a knowledge of language help you?

The answer is that language is not merely an examination subject, but an essential tool. You will use it all your life, to express yourself and communicate with other people. If you want to use it well — that is, clearly, accurately and without being misunderstood — you first have to know how language is made up. You should understand its different parts. One part is the words themselves, or *vocabulary* — the smallest units of language. The other main part is the *grammar* — the rules which show you how the words fit correctly together in a sentence. In addition you must be proficient in spelling and punctuation, because language is not only spoken, but also read and written.

This book explains these aspects of language and tests you, by exercises and revision sections, on what you have learned. Take care to read all the instructions thoroughly and follow them exactly.

TO THE TEACHER

The Language action approach which CSEC favours does not mean that grammar must not be taught. It simply implies the need for the *functional* use of grammar which is a characteristic of this book. The rules of grammar must be followed if students must express themselves appropriately and write effectively. You will undoubtedly have to deal with students from different backgrounds speaking various forms of dialect. While we appreciate and value creole English — which may even be appropriate in certain situations — the emphasis of this book is on Standard English in which the examination is set. This text offers the necessary guidance to the teacher who wishes to use his professional skill in intervening at the point where the student needs assistance.

This text is not an examination crammer designed only for forms 4 and 5. It lays the foundation with simple grammatical structures and gradually builds up into the more complex ones; thus making it not only student friendly but teacher friendly as well.

CONTENTS

======= LESSON 1 =======

SENTENCES AND PHRASES

When people speak or write they arrange their words in groups, to convey their message. Single words, such as *land, people, work,* cannot by themselves make much sense. They need to be correctly fitted together to make a sentence:

Many people in the Caribbean Islands work on the land.

Now we have a complete message, which tells us a fact. A sentence, therefore, is defined as *a group of words which makes complete sense.*

1. Every sentence is made up of two essential parts. Together, the two parts, called subject and predicate, provide the full meaning of the sentence.

   subject
   which tells us whom or what the sentence is about

   predicate
   which says something about the subject

   If we look again at the sentence above, we can divide it like this:

   subject
   Many people in the Caribbean Islands
   (the persons we are speaking about)

   predicate
   work on the land
   (informs us what they do)

2. Not all sentences are arranged in exactly this order. Here is a sentence with a different pattern:

   In some areas the winds blow from an easterly direction.

   subject
   the winds
   (the thing we are speaking about)

   predicate
   in some areas blow from an easterly direction
   (informs us where and how they occur)

3. You will notice that each predicate contains a verb, or action word (work, lasts). We shall study verbs more fully in Lessons 11, 12 and 13. To help you recognise a verb in a predicate, some

6

verbs are shown in italics in the following sentences:

subject	predicate
Errol	*wrote* a letter.
That dog	*is* dangerous.
Most of the pupils	*passed* their examination.
My grandmother	*made* a dress for my sister.
I	*played* my favourite record.

4. Sometimes you will find that the subject of a sentence is not the person or thing carrying out the action, but the person or thing *acted upon*.

subject	predicate
The letter	*was written* by Errol.
The house	*was built* by the Carib Construction Company.
We	*were surprised* by his sudden appearance.

5. At other times, you will find sentences where there is apparently no action, but you can still divide them into subject and predicate.

subject	predicate
This book	*is* Larry's.
The old man	*died*.
Thomas	*has* a fever.

6. As we saw earlier, the subject of a sentence is not always found at the beginning. It is possible to say:

Over went the ship. *or* The ship went over.
Down came the rain. *or* The rain came down.

In each case the division into subject and predicate is the same:

subject	predicate
The ship	*went* over.
The rain	*came* down.

7. You may even come across sentences that seem to have no subject, because the subject is 'you', though it is not actually stated:

Go to the hospital immediately.

subject	predicate
(You)	*go* to the hospital immediately.

7

8. Other sentences may seem to have no predicate. Again, you will have to imagine the words that are understood, though not stated. Here is an example:

After the riot the enquiry.

subject   **predicate**
The enquiry   (*will be held*) after the riot.

SETTING OUT A SENTENCE

All sentences must begin with a capital letter and end with a *full stop*, *a question mark* or an *exclamation mark*:

Thieves came and stole the money.
Did they get away?
I'm afraid so!

TYPES OF SENTENCE

Sentences belong to one of six types:

1. **Statement**   Errol opened the door.
Bananas are grown in the Windward Islands.

2. **Question**   Why are you here?
Where is the book?

3. **Command**   Go and wash your face.
Press the switch.

4. **Request**   Please close the door.
May I speak to the doctor.

5. **Desire or Hope** l wish I could fly direct to Miami.
He hopes to be back tomorrow.

6. **Exclamation**   How smart you look!
What a terrible storm we had last night!

PHRASES

Phrases are not the same as sentences. They are groups of words which, when put together, have *some* meaning, but *not a complete* meaning. Unlike sentences, phrases cannot be divided into subject and predicate. Look at these phrases:

in the morning   without a word
every Tuesday   across the desert
surrounded by tall trees by his side
waiting for a friend   heavily loaded
lonely and miserable   at the airport

8

None of these phrases can stand on its own. To have a full meaning it must become part of a sentence. For example:

The music teacher visits our school *every Tuesday*.
We could see a small house *surrounded by tall trees*.
The boy said he was *waiting for a friend*.
At the airport some new runways have been built.

Phrases are of various types and perform the functions of nouns, adjectives or adverbs, which we shall meet in Lesson 2.

EXERCISES

1. Write down the subject of each of these sentences:
(a) Barbados became an independent country on November 30th, 1966.
(b) Here comes the bus.
(c) When did the war end?
(d) The police remained calm during the disturbance.
(e) Will you please lend me your dictionary?

2. State what kind of sentence each of the following is:
(a) Why did you steal from the shop?
(b) Will you please put the receiver down.
(c) He was always watching the television.
(d) I hope to get to my office in forty minutes.
(e) What a terrible journey we had this morning!
(f) Come back at once.

3. State the subjects and the predicates in these sentences:
(a) Sam Lord lived in a castle in Barbados.
(b) Here is the manager.
(c) Mrs Thomas bought some mangoes in the market.
(d) When did you see the doctor?
(e) Don't go too near the river bank.
(f) Why are you here?

4. For each of these subjects choose the most suitable predicate from those given:

subjects	predicates
The mechanic	has three sides.
Further information	help to keep law and order.
Montego Bay	removed the plugs.
October	can be obtained from the office.
The police	is in the North of Jamaica.
A triangle	comes after September.

5. Answer these questions with a statement:
(a) What is the chief town of Trinidad?
(b) What is your favourite subject?
(c) Where do you live?
(d) Which television programme do you like best?
(e) Why are you reading this book?

6. Suggest questions which fit these answers:
(a) We expect another delivery next week.
(b) I've had a pain in my side for three weeks.
(c) The highest temperature recorded in Barbados was in August last year.
(d) Both my sisters are married.

7. State which of the following are sentences and which are phrases:

(a) In the library	(e) Very close to the wall
(b) Termites cause a lot of damage	(f) By this time
(c) Speak clearly	(g) I am reading a novel by E.R. Braithwaite
(d) Rubbing his hands	(h) To the promised land

8. Use one of these phrases to complete each of the sentences below:

as quickly as possible	all the same
on the other hand	right from the start
through and through	for enlarging objects

(a) Cole was easily the best runner. He led the race ....
(b) This order is urgent. Please send me the goods ....
(c) A microscope is ....
(d) You could tell at once that the girl was a Barbadian. She was a Barbadian ....
(e) You may be right, but .... I am sticking to my opinion.
(f) .... if we don't increase taxes there will be no money to pay the teachers.

PARTS OF SPEECH

Words are classified into *parts of speech*, according to their function in a sentence. There are eight parts of speech:

1. Nouns
2. Verbs
3. Pronouns
4. Adjectives

5. Adverbs
6. Prepositions
7. Conjunctions
8. Interjections

You will meet them briefly in this lesson and study them in more detail in the later lessons of the book.

A word, however, may be classed as more than one part of speech, depending on the way it is used. In these examples, the word 'fast' has *four* different functions and is therefore *four* different parts of speech:

(a) He will *fast* during Lent.   (verb)
(b) After Lent the *fast* ended.   (noun)
(c) He works *fast*.   (adverb)
(d) Charles is a *fast* worker.   (adjective)

By looking carefully at the function the word performs in the sentence we can decide what part of speech it is. Here are the functions of the parts of speech, with examples:

1. **Nouns** are words that name *persons, places, things* or *ideas:*

    Mrs Jones   Nassau   sugar   independence

2. **Pronouns** are words used instead of nouns:

    I   they   she   he   it

    These words save us from having to repeat too often the names of persons and things when we speak or write. Consider the following sentence:

    Mr Ramsammy told Mrs Harris that Mr Ramsammy would be pleased to see Mrs Harris at eleven o'clock.

    A better way of saying this is:

    Mr Ramsammy told Mrs Harris that *he* would be pleased to see *her* at eleven o'clock.

11

3. **Verbs**, as we have already seen in Lesson 1, are words of *doing, being, having, saying* or *thinking*. They usually involve *action* by the subject of the sentence:

I *remember*.   She *believes*.
Birds *fly*.   The government *decides*.

Verbs can also express circumstances:

Sam *seems* happy today.
Our neighbour *became* ill.

Verbs, because they express action, often have an effect upon something, or somebody, and this thing or person is called the *object* of the verb:

She dropped the plate.	(verb *dropped*; object *plate*)
The teacher marks my book.	(verb *marks*; object *book*)
Father crossed the road.	(verb *crossed*; object *road*)
I recognised the girl.	(verb *recognised*; object *girl*)

Remember that *not all verbs take objects*. This point is discussed more fully in Lesson 11.

4. **Adjectives** give us more information about nouns or pronouns:

a *wild* animal; a *poisonous* snake; a *clever* politician; He was *angry*.

5. **Adverbs** give us more information about a verb, an adjective or another adverb. They answer the questions *how? when? where? why? to what degree or extent?* Here are some examples:

The band played *loudly*.	(describing the verb *played*, and answering the question *how?*)
She was *extremely* attractive.	(describing the adjective *attractive* and answering the question *to what degree?*)
He was going *too* fast.	(describing the adverb *fast* and answering the question *to what degree?*)

Many adverbs are formed from adjectives by adding the ending (also known as the suffix) *-ly*, as in slow, *slowly*; close, *closely*; gracious, *graciously*.

12

6. **Prepositions** are words placed before a noun or pronoun to show a connection with some other word in the sentence:

> in through with over under of about across before along against inside.

They may link a noun with a verb, adjective, noun or pronoun:

> The ship sailed *across* the ocean. (linking *sailed* and *ocean*)
>
> Cold *from* exposure, James covered himself *with* a blanket. (linking *cold* and *exposure*; linking *himself* and *blanket*)
>
> Mohammed was the leader *of* the party. (linking *leader* and *party*)

7. **Conjunctions** are joining words: *and, but, so*. See Lesson 18.

8. **Interjections** are usually single words, such as exclamations or expressions of sudden feeling. They may also express agreement or disagreement:

> Indeed! Nonsense! Congratulations!
> Hello! Sorry! Certainly!

USING YOUR DICTIONARY

The names of the parts of speech are usually abbreviated (shortened) in referring to words in a dictionary. It is important when looking up a word in a dictionary to note what part of speech it is. The following are the abbreviations:

verb	v.	adverb	adv.
noun	n.	preposition	prep.
pronoun	pron.	conjunction	conj.
adjective	adj.	interjection	int.

Here are some examples:

drill	n.	a tool for making holes
	v.	to make holes
expert	adj.	skilful, having knowledge
	n.	a person with a special knowledge or skill
round	adj.	circular
	n.	a regular route (postman's round)
	prep.	in a circular movement (the earth moves round the sun)
	adv.	moving in a circular manner (the ship turned round)

13

EXERCISES

1. Write down the part of speech of each word in italics in these sentences:

(a) He *bought* some potatoes in the market.
(b) The river is *muddy* because of the rains.
(c) *Vegetables* fetch high prices in the markets.
(d) He ran *swiftly* along the street.
(e) A foreigner has to have a residence permit if *he* wishes to stay in the country.
(f) It was a hot *and* humid night.
(g) Will you give 50 cents *to* this poor man?
(h) *Really*! That is not a polite thing to do.
(i) I would like to go to the speech day, *but* I have another engagement.
(j) *Mr Khan* is a clerk in Georgetown.
(k) They live *here* for part of the year.

2. The same word can be more than one part of speech. State the part of speech of each word in italics:

(a) John was put in the *care* of his grandmother.
(b) I do not *care* what happens.
(c) I *long* to get away from the city.
(d) There are shops on both sides of this *long* street.
(e) Will you be *long*?
(f) I would like to *book* two seats for tonight's concert.
(g) This *book* is by a well known Caribbean author.
(h) The *witness* said he thought the driver was at fault.
(i) If you *witness* an accident you must report it to the police.

3. Write down the pronouns in the following sentences:

(a) Many school leavers cannot find jobs because they do not have good qualifications.
(b) He stopped the car when it began to make a peculiar noise.
(c) Ours is the best house in the street.
(d) Several countries export bananas, and Grenada is one of them.

4. From the list of adjectives choose a suitable word to fill each of the spaces in the sentences below:

   basic   deep   approximate   powerful   uninhabited
   generous   expensive

(a) The chairman made a .... gift to the local hospital.

14

(b) The teacher told me to give an .... answer.

(c) The wheels of the truck left a .... track in the soft mud.

(d) You could tell the hut was .... because there was no smoke.

(e) The .... aim of the plan is to increase the productivity of the firm.

(f) The turbine was driven by a .... engine.

(g) Tourist rates in the winter are more ....

5. From the list of verbs choose a suitable word to fill each of the spaces in the sentences below:

   assure   collapsed   reverse   borrow   encouraged

(a) The bridge .... when the river overflowed its banks.

(b) The headmaster .... us to sit for the CXC examination.

(c) You can .... only two books at a time.

(d) 'I .... you it's quite safe,' said the guide.

(e) If you cannot go forward, ... the car.

6. Indicate the adverbs in the following sentences. Say what word each adverb describes and the part of speech of that word:

(a) I studied hard at the university.

(b) Work in the factories is very strenuous.

(c) He was swimming too fast for the others to catch up.

(d) She rudely slammed the door in my face.

7. Indicate the prepositions and conjunctions in these sentences:

(a) He was not badly hurt, but he cut his knee on a stone.

(b) Engineering courses are available at the St. Augustine Campus of the U.W.I in Trinidad and courses in medicine are available at the Mona Campus in Jamaica.

(c) Put the glass on the table when you have finished drinking.

8. In each of these sentences the word in italics is incorrect because it is the wrong part of speech. Give the correct word and say what part of speech it is:

(a) They *complaint* of the noise.

(b) Ruimveldt is an *industry* estate.

(c) He can do the work as *good* as I.

(d) I walked *pass* the market.

(e) The damaged car *obstruction* the road.

(f) He *past* the examination.

(g) They then *weight* our luggage.

LESSON 3

VOCABULARY

The word *vocabulary* refers to, or is used to describe, the number and variety of words with which a person is familiar and which he or she is able to use correctly. People's vocabularies naturally vary as much as their character or appearance. Vocabulary depends largely on education, occupation and surroundings. For example, a doctor, a farmer and a university lecturer have their own different vocabularies. Professional workers need special words related to their professions. New words are continually being created, for example:

computer astronaut count-down transistor hijack multinational hit-man microfilm videotape

CHOOSING THE RIGHT WORD AND KNOWING THE MEANING

Good use of words, whether you are speaking or writing, depends on choosing those with very clear and appropriate meanings. You are studying English grammar in order to be able to use words correctly. You will, therefore, have to know the meanings of the words you use. This involves learning to use the dictionary properly. In English one word may mean *almost*, but not exactly, the same thing as some other word. The following pairs of words, for example, are similar, but they are not quite the same in meaning:

small	microscopic	understand	sympathise
anonymous	unknown	remember	memorise
immaculate	clean	ecstatic	happy
pain	discomfort	story	myth
damage	devastate	terrify	scare

Find out the differences by using your dictionary. Your teacher should be able to help you.

INCREASING YOUR VOCABULARY

To acquire the right new words — that is, to keep on increasing your vocabulary — you should read about new things every day, using encyclopaedias, reference books, textbooks, newspapers, good quality magazines and novels. Always take note of the words with which people, places or things are described.

When you leave school you are expected to be familiar with a range of vocabulary, which is wide enough to allow you to read with understanding, or write with confidence, on topics of general interest. These topics might include, for example, trade and commerce, transport and communications, government and politics, sports and entertainment, manufacturing industries, building and construction, agriculture and rural life. Think of some jobs and occupations that have their own specialised vocabulary. Think of your particular leisure-time interests and the words connected with them. Once you become really aware of words, and notice each new one you meet, your vocabulary is certain to build up.

EXERCISES

1. From each of the following pairs of words choose the one you consider better for ordinary everyday use. Use the word in a sentence to show its precise meaning:

approximately	...about	encounter	...meet
singer	...vocalist	assist	...help
commence	...begin	try	...endeavour
wealthy	...affluent	consume	...eat
category	...class	dwelling	...home
neighbourhood	..vicinity	agriculturist	..farmer
donate	...give	clever	...ingenious
bruise	...contusion	convey	...send

2. In the sentences below, the words in italics are incorrect. From the following list of words choose the correct word for each sentence:

    borrowed installed far take hurt destroyed congested
    number showed extravagant

    (a) The house is very *distant* from the road.
    (b) He was knocked down by a car and badly *harmed*.
    (c) I *lent* a book from the library.
    (d) A guide *led* us the way.
    (e) People who spend a lot on their children are *luxurious*.
    (f) The government should limit the *amount* of cars imported into Jamaica.
    (g) Those overhead lights were *established* last year.
    (h) It will *cost* you half an hour.
    (i) Flyovers would prevent the roads being *condensed*.
    (j) Many trees were *destructed* by fire.

3. Find simpler words to use instead of the following:

    terminate initiate decease ultimate odour
    conversationalist naive nefarious irrigate

4. The words *say, ask, speak, tell* and *talk* are sometimes confused. Choose the correct part of the correct verb (for example, *speak — speaking*) to fill each of the spaces in the following sentences:

(a) Miss Joseph, our teacher, ... , 'Do not start the exercise until I .... you.'
(b) Joe wasn't .... the truth when he explained why he was absent.
(c) 'What were you .... about when I came in?' .... Judy.
(d) What other languages can you .... ?
(e) I don't understand what you are ....
(f) I would understand if you .... sense.
(g) He is so often late for school I shall have to .... to him.
(h) Mr Singh is .... to be very mean.

5. Find the correct word from the following lists to fill the numbered spaces in the passages below. Decide what function each missing word has in the sentence — for example, is it a verb, a noun, an adjective or adverb? Then, if you are not sure of the meaning of a word, look it up in your dictionary.

(a) sensational   victim   acquitted   benefactor   evident
     charged   established   savage

When Sir Harry Oakes, a great ...1... to the Island of New Providence, was found dead early one morning in 1943 it was ...2... that he had been the ...3... of a ...4... murder. His son-in-law was ...5... with the murder and later ...6... after a ...7... trial. The truth about the murder has never been ...8... .

create   responsible   legendary   disunited   freedom
object   exploits   republic   realised   capture

(b) Bolívar's ...1... for the ...2... of South America are ...3... . He led troops across the Andes to ...4... Bogota and was ...5... for freeing not only Venezuela, but Columbia, Peru and Ecuador. His ...6... was to ...7... a self-governing ...8... of a number of nations, but this aim was never ...9... . The nations became free, but ...10... .

portray   completion   culture   revived   celebrate

(c) The ...1... of Bajan society is still ...2... in Cropover, a festival to ...3... the ...4... of the cane harvest in which scores of costumed bands ...5... anything from Arawak Indians to a game of cricket, as they march and dance from the National Stadium.

(d) confined obliging favour periphery designated

Mr Bernard said he was in ...1... of making Port of Spain a no-parking area for private motor cars, ...2... everybody to park on the ...3... of the city and use public buses into and through the city. Taxis would be ...4... to well ...5... stands.

6. From the list of nouns below referring to people, select for each of the following descriptions the word that fits it best:

inmate shop-lifter teetotaller addict hooligan broker genius

(a) Someone who never drinks alcohol.
(b) Someone who takes something from a shop without paying for it.
(c) Someone who is exceptionally clever.
(d) Someone who constantly takes too much of a drug and cannot live without it.
(e) Someone who arranges a sale for another person.
(f) Someone who lives in an institution.
(g) Someone who is rude, selfish and violent.

7. From the list of words below referring to speech, select for each of the following sentences the correct one to fill the space:

warned announced pronounce refute sermon declared remonstrating advised address

(a) The preacher gave a .... about the wickedness of accepting bribes.
(b) When charged with the offence, the prisoner steadfastly .... his innocence.
(c) I .... him not to go too fast on the motor-bike.
(d) Mr and Mrs Rodriguez .... the date of their daughter's wedding.
(e) I cannot .... this word correctly.
(f) The principal gave an inspiring .... to the whole school.
(g) I .... him to put his money in the bank.
(h) It was no use .... with him; he was determined to go his own way.
(i) I could not .... his argument because it seemed faultless.

============ LESSON 4 ============

NOUNS
Types of noun

Nouns, which we have already met in Lesson 2, are *naming* words, and they are of four different types:

1. COMMON NOUNS

These are names given to persons or things that we often come across in everyday life. They are called common because they are *common to* (which means *shared by*) many persons or things:

> boy ship school road town animal woman mountain

2. PROPER NOUNS

A proper noun names a *particular* person, place or thing:

> Garfield Sobers   The Prime Minister   Vice-President   Dr Perot
> Dominica   St Michael's Cathedral   the Equator   Black River

The word *proper* comes from a Latin word meaning *own*. Remember this and it will help you to decide whether a noun is a proper noun. A noun with its *own special qualities* that make it different from other nouns of the same class is a proper noun. Your *own* name is a proper noun and so are the days of the week and the months of the year. Proper nouns are always written with a capital letter.

3. COLLECTIVE NOUNS

A collective noun is used for a *group* or *collection*. Groups are of many kinds and they may consist of people, animals or objects. Here are some examples of collective nouns:

herd	= some/many animals	nation	= many citizens
flock	= some/many birds	staff	= some/many workers
pack	= some/many cards	workforce	= some/many workers
gang	= some/many robbers	audience	= some/many listeners
crowd	= many people	class	= some/many pupils
army	= many soldiers	vocabulary	= many words

family	= some/many relations	forest	= many trees
fleet	= some/many ships	orchestra	= many players

It is not possible to give a list of all the collective nouns. You should look out for them in your reading and be able to recognise them. A collective noun usually has a *singular verb* because it is considered as *one unit*; but if you are discussing the *separate members* who make up the unit, then a plural verb is needed. You will learn more about singular and plural in Lesson 5. Look at these examples:

The committee demands (singular verb) more money for education.

The committee were divided (plural verb) in their opinions.

The government has announced (singular verb) new measures to help farmers.

The government were unable (plural verb) to agree on a policy.

However, as the next examples show, you are likely to need a singular verb more often than a plural verb:

The herd was moving along slowly.
The flock flies south.
The gang was caught by the police.
The nation is shocked by the news.
The army needs more weapons.
The fleet of tankers is waiting in the harbour.

4. ABSTRACT NOUNS

These nouns are used for the names of qualities, conditions, emotions and actions. The word *abstract* means something that is outside the physical world of things that we see, hear, touch, taste and smell. Abstract nouns, therefore, are *connected with ideas and feelings*. Look at these examples:

goodness	education	sorrow	honesty
health	cruelty	selfishness	friendship
anger	patience	brotherhood	bravery
truthfulness	justice	attraction	sympathy

EXERCISES

1. Read the passage below, then write out:

(a) all the common nouns in it;
(b) all the proper nouns in it.

Applications are invited for a post as foreman in building construction. Candidates should have a good background in carpentry

21

and at least five years' experience. Write to the General Manager, Sunspot Builders, P.O. Box 1998, Freeport, Grand Bahama.

2. Find the proper nouns in the following sentences and write them out *correctly*, using capital letters where necessary:

(a) The west indies jaycees will hold their annual general meeting from may 28th to may 29th. The meeting will be chaired by the president, hugh whittaker of jamaica.
(b) I have passed the cxc examination with a credit in english.
(c) I saw a new rolls-royce in port of spain last tuesday.
(d) I was reading the bible to my brother alec.
(e) Work has commenced on highway 7 from the grantley adams international airport to bridgetown, the speightstown by-pass and the belmont roundabout.

3. Choose the most suitable collective noun from the list given to complete each sentence:

crew   flight   swarm   team   pack   flock   herd

(a) Do not believe him; his whole story is a .... of lies.
(b) The pilot and other members of the .... were the last to leave the aircraft.
(c) A .... of flies settled on the dead bird.
(d) Mr Smith's office was on the first floor, up a .... of stairs.
(e) The captain of the winning .... scored 64 in the away match.
(f) A large .... of elephants could be seen along the river bank.
(g) A .... of birds flew behind the tractor, seeking food from the upturned soil.

4. Find the word for:

(a) A group of robbers
(b) A group of military musicians
(c) A vast area of trees
(d) A group of islands
(e) A group of people who work for a shop, college or firm
(f) People in a church

5. Give the abstract nouns related to the following common nouns (for example, *boy, boyhood*):

(a) friend   (c) thief   (e) partner   (g) criminal
(b) child   (d) hero   (f) coward   (h) guide

6. Give the abstract nouns related to the following adjectives:

(a) anxious   (d) wise   (g) private   (j) simple
(b) prosperous   (e) tolerant   (h) clean   (k) young
(c) proud   (f) certain   (i) poor   (l) ill

22

NOUNS
Number, Possessive Form and Gender

1. NUMBER

If a noun names a *single* person or thing it is said to be *singular* (meaning only one). If it names *more than one* person or thing it is said to be *plural*.

Nouns forming a regular plural

Most nouns form their plural by adding -s to the singular:

    day, days; book, books; head, heads; mother, mothers; river, rivers

Nouns forming an irregular plural

Some nouns do not follow the usual rule for the plural. There are several kinds:

(a) Nouns ending in -s, -ch, -sh, -x, -z and -o add -es;

    kiss, kisses; church, churches; bush, bushes; box, boxes; buzz, buzzes; mango, mangoes

(b) Some words ending in -o which came into English from other languages — and also some abbreviations — add -s to make their plural:

    piano, pianos; solo, solos; folio, folios; photo, photos; radio, radios

(c) Nouns ending in a consonant followed by -y change the -y into -ies:

    lady, ladies; baby, babies; country, countries; pony, ponies; city, cities

(d) Some nouns ending in -f or -fe change to -ves in the plural:

    wife, wives; shelf, shelves; half, halves; thief, thieves; wolf, wolves

(e) Some nouns form their plural by a vowel change:

    mouse, mice; man, men; foot, feet; tooth, teeth; goose, geese

(f) Some nouns add *-en* to make the plural:

> child, children; ox, oxen; brother, brethren (but only when referring to members of a religious society)

(g) Some nouns stay the same for both singular and plural:

> sheep, sheep; Swiss, Swiss (He is a Swiss. The Swiss are good mountaineers.)

(h) Some nouns have *no plural*:

> information, advice, news, knowledge, weather, sunshine, luggage, baggage

(i) Some nouns exist only in the plural; they have *no singular* form:

> jeans   shorts   police   cattle   scissors   trousers   pliers
> tongs   scales

(j) Nouns which have kept their Greek or Latin spelling take the Greek or Latin plural endings:

> terminus, termini; stimulus, stimuli; crisis, crises; oasis, oases; radius, radii; phenomenon, phenomena; stratum, strata; stadium, stadia

(k) Compound nouns are made by joining two or more words, as in *bedroom, eyebrow* and *football*, and these nouns vary in their plurals. Normally *-s* is added to the whole word:

> armchair, armchairs; pickpocket, pickpockets; stepfather, stepfathers; buttonhole, buttonholes

When *man* or *woman* is the first part of the compound noun, the first and second parts both change to make the plural:

> manservant, menservants; woman-teacher, women-teachers

If the compound noun contains a preposition or adverb, *only the noun part* is made plural:

> sister-in-law, sisters-in-law; passer-by, passers-by

If the compound noun has an adjective as the last word, the *first* word is usually made plural:

> court martial, courts martial

Words ending in *-ful* usually add *-s* for the plural:

> handful, handfuls; basketful, basketfuls; plateful, platefuls; spoonful, spoonfuls

2. POSSESSION

Sometimes an *apostrophe*('), pronounced aPOStrofy, is added to a noun to show ownership, or possession:

> Joe's shoes (the shoes belonging to Joe); the car's engine (the engine belonging to the car); the people's wishes (the wishes of the people)

With a *plural* noun the apostrophe is added *after* the plural ending:

> the girls' school; the OPEC ministers' decision; the babies' food; the countries' problems; the thieves' punishment; the children's party; women's hair-styles

Some proper nouns ending in *-s* do not take a further *-s* in the possessive, because the double *s* sound would be difficult to pronounce. Instead they have only the apostrophe:

> Dickens' novels; Keats' poems

Note

Where two nouns are placed together, as in *the girls' school*, the apostrophe indicates possession. In many cases where two nouns are placed together without an apostrophe there is an implied idea of possession. The first word, however, is acting as an adjective:

> the *bathroom* door; a *television* aerial; the *car* windscreen; a *clock* face; *tooth* decay; a *torch* battery; a *picture* frame; a *conservation* area; the *road* surface

The *road* surface means the 'surface of the road'. The first word *surface* may appear to be a normal noun, but here it is acting as an adjective.

3. GENDER

Every noun has its own gender and it belongs to one of four types:

(a) Masculine

These nouns are male:

> king   boy   father   bull   grandson   headmaster   lord

(b) Feminine

These nouns are female:

> queen   girl   mother   cow   granddaughter
> headmistress   lady

(c) Common

These nouns may be *either* male or female:

> baby   person   citizen   passenger   pupil   worker   teacher

(d) Neuter

These nouns are neither male nor female:

table house money field airport harbour

Note

Some masculine nouns change their ending to make the corresponding feminine noun. Here are some examples:

emperor, empress; count countess; heir, heiress; lion, lioness; god, goddess

EXERCISES

1. Give the plural of these nouns:

(a) coach	(e) agency	(i) footrest	(m) stairway
(b) duty	(f) mouse	(j) potato	(n) brush
(c) class	(g) calf	(k) bus	(o) toy
(d) son-in-law	(h) French	(l) knife	(p) memorandum

2. In these sentences correct any errors in the singular or plural of nouns:

(a) Eric has plenty of works to do.

(b) The government should provide more money for the constructions of roads.

(c) Many aircrafts land at the Grantley Adams International Airport.

(d) The rest house was built in the most beautiful surrounding.

(e) Your teacher will give you the best advices on what course to take.

(f) The factory has the most modern equipments.

(g) Television helps to spread knowledges to all the people.

(h) When the water is heated, steams rise from the container.

(i) The local people have contributed fund to equip their health centre.

(j) If you want to succeed in business you must give values for money.

(k) At the annual sale, Hodgkinson's have a wide range of article for sale.

(l) The person appointed will be responsible for the maintenance of all the laboratory apparatuses.

(m) There are two hundred known drugs which will cover the health need of most people.

(n) The politician said: 'We have built this country by our own blood, tear and sweat.'

(o) People living in rural area have been neglected.

26

3. In the following sentences the writer has mistaken a singular noun for a plural, and the verbs are therefore wrong. Re-write them as they should be:

(a) Mathematics are very difficult to learn.
(b) The population are suffering because of the drought.
(c) Measles are a dangerous disease for young children.
(d) The news were passed from one village to another.
(e) At the moment our information are unreliable.
(f) Billiards are a popular game.
(g) The United States of America are an important world power.

4. Write out each of the following, adding an apostrophe in the correct place, to indicate possession:

(a) The Boys Brigade of Guyana
(b) The ships bridge
(c) Councillor Williams visit
(d) The servants quarters
(e) The club members dining room
(f) St Johns Church
(g) The Childrens Hospital
(h) The kings accession
(i) Three years experience
(j) Jamaicas main exports

5. Write out the following nouns and indicate by the letters M, F, C or N if the noun is masculine, feminine, common or neuter:

(a) son   (e) infant   (i) ink   (m) immigrant
(b) bride   (f) murderer   (j) parent   (n) cup
(c) bull   (g) actor   (k) author   (o) student
(d) bicycle   (h) widow   (l) church   (p) oil

6. Give the feminine equivalent of:

(a) nephew   (c) tiger   (e) manager
(b) actor   (d) uncle   (f) benefactor

7. Give the masculine equivalent of:

(a) girl-friend   (c) waitress   (e) stewardess
(b) daughter-in-law (d) baroness   (f) heroine

PRONOUNS
Personal and Relative

We learned in Lesson 2 that a pronoun is used instead of a noun, and so helps us to avoid repetition.

1. PERSONAL PRONOUNS

The words *I, you, he, she, it, we* and *they* are called personal pronouns. They are divided into three groups:

(a) First person pronouns

These refer to the person or persons speaking:

I me we us

(b) Second person pronouns

These refer to the person or persons spoken to:

you

(c) Third person pronouns

These refer to the person, persons, thing or things spoken about:

he, him; she, her; it, they, them

The different forms that personal pronouns take depend on their use, which may be as:

the *subject* of a sentence (referred to as the *nominative* case)
the *object* of a sentence (referred to as the *accusative* case)
indicating *ownership* (referred to as the *genitive* or *possessive* case)

SINGULAR	Nominative	Accusative	Genitive
First person	I	me	mine
Second person	you	you	yours
Third person	he she it	him her it	his hers its
PLURAL			
First person	we	us	ours
Second person	you	you	yours
Third person	they	them	theirs

Here are some examples:

He (*third person singular nominative*) saw me (*first person singular accusative*).

28

We (*first person plural nominative*) helped them (*third person plural accusative*).

They (*third person plural nominative*) said the books were mine (*first person singular genitive*).

Faults to avoid

(a) Although it is correct to say: *It was I*, common usage allows us to say: *It was me*.
But if the sentence continues as: *It was I who drove the car*, then *I* is correct and *me* should not be used.
(b) Avoid the frequent mistake of saying: *between you and I*. You must say: *between you and me*, because the preposition *between* is followed by the accusative case.
(c) Never use an apostrophe with the genitive case. Write *theirs*, not *their's*.
(d) Do not confuse the possessive use of pronouns with the possessive adjectives (*my, your, his, her, its, our, your* and *their*) which you will meet in Lesson 8.

2. RELATIVE PRONOUNS

The most important of these are *who, whom, whose, which* and *that*. They not only take the place of a noun, but also join two parts of a sentence. For example:

Mr Francis is the manager of the Caribbean Food Company.
Mr Francis will give a lecture on food distribution at the college next Wednesday.

These two sentences can be joined as follows:

Mr Francis, *who* is the manager of the Caribbean Food Company, will give a lecture on food distribution at the college next Wednesday.

Who, Whom

The relative pronouns *who* and *whom* refer (or *relate*) to persons; *which* refers to things; *that* may refer to persons or things, especially when defining a particular person or thing.

Can you remember the name of the salesman *who* called?
Here is a book *which* I want to read.
The house *that* my grandfather built is at the end of the street.

The accusative *whom* is used after a preposition (*from, to, by, for, with,* etc.):

> the person from whom I bought the car
> the person to whom I sold the car

However, it is now acceptable in English to use a more informal construction, with the preposition moved further back in the sentence:

> the person whom I bought the car from
> the person whom I sold the car to

It is also acceptable, and certainly more usual, to leave out the relative pronoun altogether:

> the person I bought the car from

Whose

The possessive *whose* joins two parts of a sentence where one part relates to ownership or possession. For example:

> The dealers' profit ranges from fifty per cent to a hundred per cent.
> The dealers will have to bring down the cost of food.

These sentences can be combined as:

> The dealers, whose profit ranges from fifty per cent to a hundred per cent, will have to bring down the cost of food.

Position of relative pronouns

Relative pronouns should be placed close to the words to which they relate. The following sentence is not correct:

> The booklet deals with Guyana's present economy *which* will be published by *Demerara Publications* next week.

It should be written:

> The booklet, *which* will be published by *Demerara Publications* next week, deals with Guyana's present economy.

Which (special use)

Sometimes we use the relative pronoun *which* in place of an action or complete statement, for example:

> The manager was kind to his employees, *which* made him very popular.
> (*which* refers to being kind).

> They refused to settle their dispute, *which* put an end to an early hope of peace.
> (*which* refers to the refusal to settle the dispute)

30

Note

It is important to make sure that a sentence is clear in its meaning. The following sentence, for example, is badly expressed:

> It is hard work caring for sick animals, which not many people would like.

This could be better expressed as:

> Caring for sick animals is hard work and not many people would like it.

EXERCISES

1. Write out the following sentences, inserting the correct pronoun *I* or *me*:

(a) The letter was addressed to my wife and ....
(b) It is true that both Larry and .... are guilty.
(c) The form has to be signed by you and then by .... as a witness.
(d) It is .... who wrote that anonymous letter.
(e) Open the door please! It's ....

2. Complete the following sentences with the correct relative pronoun *who, whose, whom, which* or *that:*

(a) Dr Robinson, ... obituary appears in *The Guyana Chronicle* today, was educated at the University of the West Indies.
(b) This is the dog .... killed the chicken.
(c) Those .... believe in justice must make their voices heard.
(d) There is not one politician .... I can trust.
(e) This is the best hotel .... I know in St Vincent.

3. Complete these sentences, using *to whom, from whom, with whom* or *on whom;*

(a) All the friends .... the late Senator Johnson was associated met yesterday to pay tribute to his memory.
(b) Dr Singh, ... I received my certificate, is the Principal of the College.
(c) I am sure he is the same man .... I spoke in the bus.
(d) The President is the man .... all responsibility rests.

4. Complete these sentences with *in whose, from whose, to whose, upon whose* or *with whose:*

(a) The bank manager, ... judgement I relied, gave me some bad advice.
(b) The deceased, ... memory we paid our respects, was buried in Catholic Church Cemetery.

(c) Law students prefer to study in Britain, ... legal system the present West Indian laws evolved.

(d) My brother, ... friends I was staying, had gone to play cricket.

(e) The woman .... house the fire started just managed to escape in time.

5. Say what kind of pronoun each of the words in italics is:

(a) Mr Nelson called *me* into his office.

(b) This house is *ours*.

(c) Las Casas was the Spanish priest *who* worked among the Caribs and Arawaks.

(d) We must thank the President, *whose* hospitality we have so much enjoyed.

(e) It was clear the fault was *his* because he was driving on the wrong side of the road.

(f) Haiti, *which* was the first state in the world to be freed by a revolt of the slaves, became independent in 1804.

6. Join these pairs of sentences by using a relative pronoun:

(a) Thomas Warner was one of the first Englishmen to make his home in the Caribbean.
He went to live in St Kitts.

(b) The suspect alleged that the man Smith had provoked him.
Smith was the man he attacked.

(c) Barbados' main airport at Seawell is fifteen kilometres from Bridgetown. It is served by many international airlines.

(d) The shipping wharves are on the right bank of the river Demerara.
They are reached by ferry from the settlement of Vreed en Hoop.

(e) Nylon was first produced in the laboratories of the American du Pont Company in 1930.
Women's stockings were made from nylon.

(f) The school has prospered under the direction of the Principal, Mr Russell.
All the local residents have great confidence in him.

MORE ABOUT PRONOUNS

1. REFLEXIVE PRONOUNS

These pronouns *reflect* the subject of the sentence and they each contain the word *self*:

myself   yourself   himself   herself   itself   ourselves
yourselves   themselves

They are used in a sentence such as:

You should express yourself clearly in English.

Here the word *yourself* refers to the subject *you* and completes the meaning of the verb *express*.

The reflexive pronouns corresponding to the personal pronouns are:

I	myself	
you	yourself	
he	himself	**not** his-self
she	herself	
it	itself	
one	oneself	
we	ourselves	
you (plural)	yourselves	
they	themselves	**not** theirselves

Here are some examples:

She killed herself by taking an overdose of drugs.
I blame myself for not having worked hard enough.
Speaking for myself, I think the government has acted unwisely.
They think of themselves as very superior people.
'You have shown yourself to be a most unreliable witness,' said the judge.
The storm announced itself by a tremendous clap of thunder.
We are deceiving ourselves if we rely forever on imported foodstuffs.

Note

When using the impersonal reflexive pronoun *oneself*, be careful to avoid using the wrong personal pronoun in the same sentence. For example, it is not correct to write:

To give *oneself* the best seat is not the sort of thing *you* should do.

Instead of *you*, write *one*.

Here is another sentence where the pronouns have become mixed:

Talking to *oneself* is a habit *I* often indulge in.

Instead of *oneself*, write *myself*.

Reflexive pronouns can also be used simply for emphasis:

The Chairman himself handed over a cheque for $2000 to the superintendent of the Home for Handicapped Children.

In this sentence the writer draws attention to the important person by adding *himself* for emphasis.

It is incorrect to use a reflexive pronoun as a personal pronoun:

Tom and myself went to the airport.

The correct form of this sentence is:

Tom and I went to the airport.

2. INTERROGATIVE PRONOUNS

These are the pronouns used when *asking questions*:

who? which? whom? whose? what?

Like personal pronouns (see Lesson 6), relative pronouns are used in the nominative, accusative and genitive cases:

SINGULAR and PLURAL	Nominative	Accusative	Genitive
	who	whom	whose
	which	which	of which
	what	what	of what

Here are some examples:

Who is it?
To *whom* did you address the letter?
Which will you choose?
What did you say to your teacher?
Whose is that car on the other side of the street?

Note

Interrogative pronouns have the same form as relative pronouns, which you studied in Lesson 6. The difference between them is one of function. The word *who*, for example, is an *interrogative pronoun* when used in a question. It is a *relative pronoun* when it takes the place of a noun and joins two parts of a sentence.

Who is next on the list? (interrogative)
The nurse, *who* works at the hospital, is a friend of my sister. (relative)

34

3. DEMONSTRATIVE PRONOUNS

As their name indicates, the demonstrative pronouns *this, that, these, those* demonstrate, or point out, a particular person or thing. They also *take the place of a noun:*

> *This* is the best cricket ground in the Caribbean.
> *That* is the house you are looking for.
> *These* are cheaper than *those*.

Note
Do not confuse the demonstrative pronoun with the demonstrative adjective. The adjective is used *with* a noun, never by itself.

> *These* soldiers are all Cubans.   (demonstrative adjective used with the noun *soldiers*)

Compare this sentence with:

> *These* are Cubans.   (demonstrative pronoun replacing a noun, e.g., *men*)

4. INDEFINITE PRONOUNS

Indefinite pronouns are used for nouns that have not been clearly defined. They do not stand for any definite noun. Such words are:

> another   anybody   anyone   each   either   everyone
> someone   such   all   both   few   several   some

Here are some examples:

> *Everyone* agrees the minimum wage should be raised.
> *All* are invited to the laying of the foundation stone.
> When the two men were charged, *both* said they were innocent.

Note
Once again, you must be careful not to confuse the indefinite pronoun with the indefinite adjective. If it is used to *describe a noun* (and not in place of a noun) then it is an adjective:

> Please give me *some* sugar.   (adjective)
> *All* children will be admitted at half price.   (adjective)
> I have never known *such* pain.   (adjective)

EXERCISES

1. What kinds of pronoun are the words in italics?

(a) *Nobody* accepted the invitation.
(b) *What* is the registration number?
(c) *These* are better than *those*
(d) The government *itself* cannot solve the financial problems.
(e) *Whose* is this pencil?

2. Complete the following sentences by using the most suitable interrogative pronoun:

(a) .... is the matter with him?
(b) .... will propose this motion?
(c) There are two cakes left. .... do you want?
(d) .... can we depend on?

3. Make the nouns or pronouns in italics in the following sentences more emphatic by adding a reflexive pronoun:

(a) The *headmaster* went to see the boy's parents.
(b) *We* are not entirely blameless in this disgraceful affair.
(c) The *fund* will not be sufficient to pay for the repair of the parish church.
(d) Most people are keen on sport, but *I* think too much time is wasted on football and other games.
(e) *Books* cannot provide an adequate education.

4. Add a reflexive pronoun in the spaces in these sentences to complete the meaning of the verb:

(a) The prisoner killed .... by an overdose of drugs.
(b) You can pass the examination. Do not underrate ....
(c) People who swim in this river only endanger ....
(d) I consider .... quite suitable for the position.

5. Correct the mistakes in these sentences:

(a) Eric and myself attended the same school.
(b) To who shall I give this letter?
(c) Each of the winners are to be presented with medals.
(d) They dress theirselves up in the gaudiest clothes.

6. With the help of the numbered list below which gives the type of pronoun, fill each space with the correct pronoun:

1. indefinite 2. relative 3. personal 4. reflexive 5. interrogative
6. demonstrative

(a) ....1.... believed that the world was round when Columbus sailed from Spain in 1492.
(b) The solution destroys termites ....2.... cause a great deal of damage to wooden buildings.
(c) The sugar cane is taken to the factory. ....3.... is then cut and crushed by heavy rollers.
(d) The captain blamed ....4.... and no-one else for the team's failure.
(e) ....5.... are the Windward Islands?
(f) ....6.... is not the way to hold a cricket bat.

REVISION

1. State the subjects and predicates in these sentences:
(a) Carib Insurance Company has opened branch offices in St Lucia and St Vincent.
(b) Have you a bank account?
(c) Don't touch these animals.
(d) Mrs Thomson was watching the television programme.
(e) The party will be held next Wednesday.

2. Use one of these phrases to complete each of the sentences below:

   by all means   in quick succession
   of proven integrity   without permission
   for taking photogaphs   to an end

(a) Applications are invited for the post of cashier from persons ....
(b) Jamaica's colonial status came .... on 6th August, 1962.
(c) The camera is ....
(d) The gunman fired several shots ....
(e) You are not allowed to leave the examination room ....
(f) .... do as you wish.

3. Write down the part of speech of each word in italics:
(a) He *sold* his car to a friend.
(b) The company made *generous* gifts to education.
(c) These *batteries* last longer.
(d) The old man walked *slowly* up the street.
(e) *He* went to St Jago High School in 1946.
(f) Applicants should call at the bank *or* write to the manager.
(g) A driver is required *with* at least two years' experience.
(h) *Mrs Battoo* works in a bank.
(i) You can park *here* for two hours.

4. The sentences below contain proper nouns without capital letters. Write them out correctly with capital letters:
(a) They were married at st joseph's church, barbados.

(b) The *barbados advocate's* representative met the leader of the opposition at the house of assembly for this interview.

(c) The prescribed book for the examination was anthony's 'green days by the river'.

(d) The address of the caribbean examinations council is the garrison, st. michael 20, barbados, west indies.

5. Give the abstract nouns related to these common nouns and adjectives:

(a) material   (e) man   (i) broad   (m) bureaucrat
(b) charming   (f) desperate (j) poor   (n) master
(c) enchanting (g) criminal   (k) sad   (o) expert
(d) intelligent (h) Christian (l) fool   (p) innocent

6. Write out the following correctly and indicate possession, placing the apostrophe in the correct position:

(a) The soldiers quarters (soldiers – plural)
(b) The companys profit
(c) The Peoples Republic of China
(d) Five years imprisonment
(e) Two weeks course
(f) Bishops High School

7. Complete the following sentences with the correct relative pronoun from the list below:

who   whose   whom   which   that

(a) Mr Ford, ... article appeared in the newspaper last week, is president of the Chamber of Commerce.
(b) Will anyone .... witnessed the accident please inform the police.
(c) He is not a person .... I can rely on.
(d) 'This is clearly the gun .... was used by the killer,' said the detective.
(e) In their last match the team scored seven goals, ... is the highest score this year.

ADJECTIVES

We learned in Lesson 2 that adjectives give us more information (or *qualify*) nouns or pronouns. They are words which help to provide additional meaning.

If you study advertisements you will see descriptions such as:

safe tyres, *tough* shoes, *waterproof* coats, *reliable* watches, *fresh* fruit

Without these adjectives we should know far less about the goods being offered.

Adjectives are divided into the following classes:

1. ADJECTIVES OF QUALITY

These adjectives tell what sort or kind:

Our school is a *square* building.
Help me to carry this *heavy* box.
The *dry* weather is causing problems for farmers.
The *young* children stayed at home with their mothers.

Sometimes adjectives of quality look as though they are nouns (see Lesson 5). But the first word in each of the following examples answers the question 'What sort of . . . ?'

chair seat   What sort of seat?
wine merchant   What sort of merchant?
tennis ball   What sort of ball?

Similarly, adjectives of quality can be used as plural nouns when describing a class. Here is an example from the Bible:

Blessed are the *meek*. Blessed are the *merciful*.

Several other words which are usually adjectives can also indicate a class of people:

the *poor* the *old* the *rich* the *blind* the *strong*
the *underprivileged* the *deprived*

2. DEMONSTRATIVE ADJECTIVES

The demonstrative adjectives *this, that, these, those* are used before a noun and *demonstrate*, or point out, which particular persons or things you are referring to:

> *That* woman has five children.
> *Those* books are falling to pieces.

As already mentioned in Lesson 7, you should not confuse demonstrative adjectives with demonstrative pronouns, which are *not followed by a noun*:

> *This* chair is for sale.　　　　　　(demonstrative adjective)
> *This* is for sale.　　　　　　　　(demonstrative pronoun)

3. DISTRIBUTIVE ADJECTIVES

These adjectives are used to pick out members of a group of nouns. They are *each, every, either, neither*:

> *Either* day will suit me.
> *Every* teacher wants his pupils to succeed.

Note

If, however, these words are used without a noun they are not adjectives, but pronouns. The exception is *every*, which cannot be a pronoun:

> *Each* boy carried a bag.　　　　　(distributive adjective)
> *Each* carried his own bag.　　　　(distributive pronoun)

4. ADJECTIVES OF QUANTITY OR NUMBER

These adjectives tell you *how many* or *how much*:

> There were *three* glasses.
> He drank *some* water.
> *Few* people were present.

All *numbers* when used with nouns are adjectives of quantity, and so are *some, few, several, enough*, expressing an *indefinite quantity*.

5. INTERROGATIVE ADJECTIVES

These adjectives ask a question about the noun that follows them:

> *Which* way did he go?
> *What* book shall we choose?
> *Whose* clothes are these?

6. POSSESSIVE ADJECTIVES

These words, *my, your, his, her, its, our, your, their* indicate ownership. They are always followed by the name of the thing or person possessed:

> his house;　your friend;　their village;　her father;　its name;
> our family

Points to remember

1. Special care must be taken with the singular and plural of the demonstrative adjectives *this, that, these, those.*
    It is incorrect to say:

    > those kind of people
    > these sort of vegetables

    You should say:

    > *that* kind of people   or   *those* kinds of people
    > this sort of vegetable   or   *these* sorts of vegetable

    Note that in the last example *these sorts of vegetable* is grammatically correct, but more informally *these sorts of vegetables* is accepted.

2. Two or more adjectives of quality placed together before a noun must be separated by a comma if the contrast between the two adjectives is very marked. A useful test is to try putting *and* between the adjectives. If *and* sounds necessary then a comma is necessary. For example:

    > the *sudden, untimely* death of our dear mother
    > a *big black* car

3. Compound adjectives are those adjectives that are made up of more than one word:
    purpose-built   well-intentioned   air-conditioned
    single-minded

    It is important to insert the hyphen between the words forming the compound adjective.

4. Be careful not to confuse an adjective ending in *-ing* with a similar word ending in *-ed*, for example, *tiring tired; entertaining entertained.*

    > The principal's speech was most *entertaining.* (not entertained)

EXERCISES

1. List the adjectives in the following:
(a) The destructive force of a hurricane derives from the extremely strong winds, intense and sustained rains bringing widespread floods and high waves around the coastline.

(b) Nassau, with its excellent climate, modern facilities and good communications became a favoured resort for wealthy Americans.
(c) Kingston has beautiful suburbs and boasts one of the greatest natural harbours in the world. It rests on a plain surrounded by mountains of spectacular beauty.

2. Read again how adjectives are classified and state the kind of each adjective in italics in the following sentences:
(a) *Which* prize would you like to win?
(b) You can depend on *this* make of watch.
(c) There are *three* supervisors in the warehouse.
(d) Start a *new* career!
(e) *His* statement was incorrect.
(f) *Each* candidate was given a question paper.

3. State which of the words in italics are interrogative adjectives and which are interrogative pronouns:
(a) *Which* is the tallest?
(b) *Which* way did he go?
(c) *Whose* is this ticket?
(d) *Whose* car is parked here?
(e) *What* plane flies direct to Miami?
(f) *What* can you do to help?

4. Choose a suitable adjective from the list on the left to fit a noun on the right:

urgent	principle
obsolete	stream
critical	sleep
audacious	film star
shallow	engine
glamorous	message
fundamental	illness
tranquil	attack

5. From each pair of words choose the correct one to fill the space:
    confusing   confused
(a) The many different customs of the Caribbean countries are sometimes .... to a tourist.
(b) I was .... by a number of questions put to me.
    inspiring   inspired
(c) The President gave a most .... speech.
(d) The people were .... to do their best to fight for victory.

satisfying   satisfied

(e) My mother prepared a most .... meal.
(f) The policeman was not .... with the answer he got from the accused.

frightening   frightened

(g) Do not be .... by such horrible stories.
(h) The girl had a most .... experience when she was attacked by the robber.

pleasing   pleased

(i) The violinist gave a very .... performance.
(j) Most people are .... at the results of the election.

astonishing   astonished

(k) I was .... to see the man was still alive after he had fallen over the cliff.
(l) To walk fifty miles in one day is an .... achievement.

surprising   surprised

(m) The enemy were .... to see armed men approaching.
(n) The most .... event was the defeat of the West Indies team.

amusing   amused

(o) The speaker related several .... stories.
(p) The comic film kept the audience ....

exciting   excited

(q) The finish of the football match was very ....
(r) The spectators got very .... when Wanderers scored.

thrilling   thrilled

(s) This is the most .... book I have ever read.
(t) The crowd was .... by the aerobatics of the pilot.

6. Which of the following adjectives would you use to say something pleasant about a friend and which would you consider unpleasant? Make two lists, one marked PLEASANT and the other UNPLEASANT.

dignified	heartless	shabby
conceited	good-looking	unreliable
dependable	honest	ridiculous
corrupt	conscientious	mean
sulky	shrewd	arrogant
considerate	discerning	patient

THE ARTICLES

1. THE INDEFINITE ARTICLE

The words *a* and *an* are called the indefinite articles, because they do not point out any definite person or thing, but are used in a general sense. The rules are:

Use *a* before a word beginning with a consonant:

    a man, a shop, a van

before a word beginning with a vowel that sounds like a consonant:

    a university, a uniform

Use *an* before a word beginning with a vowel:

    an office, an African, an examination

before a word beginning with a silent *h*:

    an hour, an heirloom

2. THE DEFINITE ARTICLE

The definite article *the* refers to a particular, or defined, person or thing:

    the government; the month of August; the principal exports; the concrete structure

The difference between the two articles

This is shown by the following examples:

    She is *a* teacher.   (no particular teacher)
    She is *the* teacher who takes us for mathematics.
                               (one particular teacher)

Points to remember

1. The indefinite article is *not* used before uncountable nouns, such as *luggage* and *advice*. Some of these nouns may be used as adjectives, as in *a luggage label, an advice note*, and here they take the indefinite article.

    The word *knowledge* is uncountable, but when it is used in a particular sense it takes the indefinite article, as in *a knowledge of mathematics*.

2. The definite article is *not* used:

   (a) before abstract nouns, except where there is a particular meaning:

     They fought for freedom.
     Zoo animals lack *the* freedom of the wild.

   (b) before plural nouns which are not specific, but *general*:

     Laws are essential for the maintenance of order.
     Pupils must obey school regulations.

EXERCISES

1. Complete the following sentences, filling each space with *a* or *an*:

(a) I had .... egg for breakfast.
(b) The train was .... hour late.
(c) The patient was taken in .... ambulance.
(d) If you work hard you may win .... scholarship to .... university.
(e) .... honest man would not do such a thing.

2. Correct the following by putting in the word *a, an* or *the* where it has been left out:

(a) I should like to be engineer.
(b) We get great deal of food from other countries.
(c) In Jamaica majority of people are engaged in agriculture.
(d) I would be happiest student in the class if I gained certificate.
(e) The most important person in Haiti is President.
(f) Do not speak to driver while bus is going along.
(g) I waited long time at bus stop.
(h) Put coin in slot before pressing button.
(i) My sister is now university student.

3. In the following sentences an unnecessary article has been inserted. Re-write each sentence, omitting this article:

(a) The library is open all the week including the Sunday.
(b) I received a news from Grenada about the riots.
(c) The teacher gave me a help with my mathematics paper.
(d) The people all over the world have the same basic human rights.
(e) I am too busy — I have a work to do.
(f) The captain received an information about the enemy.

4. Put, *a, an* or *the* in the spaces in these dialogues:

(a) There's .... man waiting to see you.
Who is he?
I think he's .... man from .... insurance company.

(b) There's .... vacancy advertised in .... *Nassau Guardian*.
What's it for?
It's for .... private secretary.
What are .... qualifications?
.... secretarial diploma and .... ability to speak Spanish.

(c) Will you buy me .... newspaper when you go shopping?
Of course, which one?
Either .... *Guardian* or .... *Tribune*.

(d) What's on at .... Globe?
I think it's .... crime film.
Not .... *Day of the Cobra*?
Yes, it's .... exciting film.

5. In the following sentences choose the correct word or words to fill the gap:

(a) .... is the cause of most nervous diseases.
    A   A fear   B   The fear   C   Fear

(b) I have .... of crossing the road.
    A   The fear   B   A fear   C   Fear

(c) The government is determined to put a stop to all forms of
    A   Waste   B   A waste   C   The waste

(d) 'That's .... of good food,' said Mother to Daniel.
    A   Waste   B   The waste   C   A waste

(e) Hepatitis is .... of the liver.
    A   The disease   B   Disease   C   A disease

(f) .... which most affected the West Coast of Africa was malaria
    A   Disease   B   A disease   C   The disease

COMPARISON OF ADJECTIVES

When an adjective is used to *compare* two things or persons, its usual (or *positive*) form may change:

This car is *faster* than that one.

Faster is called the **comparative** of the adjective *fast*.

If more than two things or persons are compared, the ending *-est* may be added to the adjective:

Philip was the *fastest* of the six runners.

Fastest is the **superlative** of the adjective *fast*.

The rule is that one-syllable adjectives form their comparative and superlative by adding *-er* and *-est*. However, adjectives of three or more syllables do not follow this rule. Their comparative is formed by using the words *more* and *most* before the adjective:

big, bigger, biggest;
interesting, more interesting, most interesting

Two-syllable adjectives make their comparative or superlative in either of these two ways. Those ending in *-ful* or *-re* usually take *more* and *most*;

careful, more careful, most careful;
obscure, more obscure, most obscure

Those ending in *-er -y* or *-ly* usually take the *-er* and *-est* form:

lazy, lazier, laziest;   clever, cleverer, cleverest;
silly, sillier, silliest

IRREGULAR COMPARISONS

Some adjectives have irregular forms, and these must be specially learned:

Positive	Comparative	Superlative
good	better	best
bad	worse	worst
much (many)	more	most
little	less	least
old	older (elder)*	older (eldest)*

*referring to people, not things

Note

1. Be careful not to use the comparative when more than two things or persons are being compared. It is wrong to say:

    Which language do you find *more difficult* — Spanish, French or German?

    The correct way to say this is:

    Which language do you find *most difficult*. . .?

    Similarly, avoid using the superlative when the comparative is required. It is wrong to say:

    Who is *slowest*, William or John?

    Here only two persons are being compared, so you must say:

    Who is *slower*. . .?

2. A mistake which is sometimes found is the 'double comparative' or 'double superlative', such as *more taller* or *most tallest*. If you follow the rules you will not make this error.

3. Certain adjectives cannot be compared. These are called *absolute adjectives*. Examples are *golden, unique, perfect, circular*. If something is described as *unique* it is the only one of its kind and nothing can be compared with it. If a table is described as *circular* it would be impossible to say that another table is 'more circular'. A table is either circular or not circular. If something is *perfect*, it is absolutely faultless and cannot be bettered. It would be impossible to say 'more perfect', or 'less perfect'.

    In all cases of absolute adjectives you should use common sense in deciding if there is a degree of comparison.

4. Comparison of two persons or things is often made by using the construction *as* .... *as* with the positive form of the adjective:

    He is *as* clever *as* his brother.

    The comparative form of the adjective is followed by *than*, when two things or persons are being compared:

    This car is faster *than* the other.

    The construction *the* .... *of* (or *in*) is used where three or more things or persons are being compared:

    This is *the* finest hour *of* my life.
    It is *the* tallest building *in* New York.

EXERCISES

1. Write complete sentences by using the correct form of the adjective which is given in the left-hand column:

(a) tall — Carlos was the .... of the two men.

(b) expensive — The meal was .... than I expected.

(c) glorious — The .... day in Britain during 1981 was the day of the Royal Wedding.

(d) thin — She was the .... child in the class.

(e) wide — This year's model is slightly .... than last year's.

(f) valuable — This diamond is outstanding; it is the .... of them all.

(g) less — He did not know the .... thing about it.

(h) attractive — I do not know which of the two hats is the ....

(i) careful — The problem of drug addiction requires the .... handling.

2. Write out in full the degrees of comparison of the following adjectives. Use the headings **Positive, Comparative, Superlative**:

near	different	happy	weak
cruel	polite	sad	vague
bad	busy	able	shrewd
great	thirsty	careless	inconclusive
hungry	wet	industrious	useful

3. Correct these sentences:

(a) George took the biggest of the two mangoes.

(b) Earl is more thin than his brother.

(c) Tie the thickest end of the rope to the post.

(d) This is the beautifullest picture I have ever seen.

(e) Children are usually more noisier than adults.

(f) This essay is worst than the one you wrote yesterday.

(g) Which footballer is the most interesting to watch — Leo or Errol?

VERBS

Look back at Lesson 2 and re-read the section on verbs.

TRANSITIVE VERBS

A verb is called *transitive* when it has an object. The object is the person or thing affected by the action from the verb:

The boy broke a *window*.

Here the action of the verb *broke* has affected a window. Therefore *window* is the object and the verb is transitive.

INTRANSITIVE VERBS

A verb is called *intransitive* when it has no object:

The enemy fled.

Here the verb *fled* has not affected any other person or thing, so it is intransitive.

Points to remember

1. The same verb may be transitive or intransitive, depending on how it is used in a sentence:

    The man *shouted*. (intransitive)
    The man *shouted* insults. (transitive)

2. Objects of verbs are of two kinds. The first kind is the *direct object* which we saw in the first example above — *window*. The second kind is the *indirect object*, which applies to a person or thing indirectly affected. The following sentence contains both kinds of object:

    Mr Harris gave *me* (indirect object) a *pen* (direct object).

    Here the indirect object means 'to me' and answers the question *to whom?* Other indirect objects answer the questions *to what? for whom? for what?*

3. Turn back to page 13 and read the paragraph about abbreviations which appear in dictionaries for the parts of speech. In some dictionaries, the verb is marked *v.t. and i.* This means *verb, transitive and intransitive*.

Verbs that are marked *v.i.* are intransitive verbs only.
Verbs that are marked *v.t.* are transitive only.
Here are some examples:

loathe	*v.t.*	to feel disgust for
rise	*v.i.*	to go up
roar	*v.t. and i.*	to make a loud noise

Check with your dictionary the abbreviations which are given after the following verbs:

happen mislead contaminate burn marry continue commit react

ACTIVE and PASSIVE

A verb is said to be *active* when its subject is performing the action of the verb:

The judge *awarded* a prize to Luke.
(subject: The judge)

A verb is said to be *passive* when the subject is *not* performing the action, but being acted upon by someone or something else:

The prize *was awarded* to Luke by the judge.
(subject: The prize)

The passive form of the verb is frequently used in orders, rules, regulations, public information, and in general where there is an *indefinite someone* or number of *people not specifically named*. In all the following examples the subject has the action done to it by an un-named body or number of people:

Applications are invited for vacant posts at the Bahamas Electricity Corporation.
Parking in the street is prohibited.
The accounts have been prepared.
Costs were awarded to the plaintiff.

EXERCISES

1. Express these sentences in the passive:
(a) We do not accept cheques.
(b) Antigua's desalination plant provides extra water supply.
(c) The governor urged the rebels to lay down their arms.
(d) Nobody must remove the books from the reading room.
(e) People all over the world watched the Royal Wedding film.

2. Express these sentences in the active form:

(a) The train was delayed by a signal failure.
(b) The final of the West Indian tennis championship was witnessed by a large crowd of spectators.
(c) French is still spoken by some of the people in the North.
(d) The rioters were dispersed by the use of C.S. gas.
(e) The robbers were trapped by a large contingent of police.

3. Write out the direct objects of the transitive verbs in these sentences:

(a) The factory at Longdenville manufactures bricks.
(b) Spaniards brought back stories of gold.
(c) He speaks English without a trace of accent.
(d) The governor's order to clear the streets angered the people.
(e) The news of the terrible murder shocked the local inhabitants.

4. Write out the indirect object of the transitive verbs in these sentences:

(a) The cashier handed Mr Gibson a receipt.
(b) Perhaps you would kindly tell me what I have done wrong.
(c) The management told the employees the decision of the directors.
(d) My neighbour sold me his three-year-old Mercedes.
(e) This experience taught us a lesson we shall not easily forget.
(f) The company had not paid them a dividend for several years.

5. The following sentences all contain an error in the use of passive and active forms. Write them out correctly.

(a) The book is consisted of twelve chapters.
(b) I told him that the watch was belonged to me.
(c) He is failed in the C.X.C. examination
(d) Oil products can divide into three kinds.
(e) It must have stolen by one of the staff.
(f) The question is easy to be answered.
(g) In spite of all efforts the traffic problem in Kingston still cannot solve.

MORE ABOUT VERBS

MOODS

The word *mood*, from a Latin word meaning manner, refers to the way in which a verb expresses a statement.

The **indicative** mood makes a factual statement or asks a question:

Havana *is* the capital of Cuba.
Puerto Ricans *play* baseball.
Will the Prime Minister *resign*?

The **imperative** mood expresses a command or request:

Don't come any nearer.
Hurry up.
Please *sign* your name here.

The **subjunctive** mood expresses conditions, wishes, uncertainties:

Whatever he *may think,* I know the real truth.
If only I *had passed* the examination, I would have got the job.

TENSES

Verbs have *tenses* which show us the time at which an action takes place.

(a) The present tense: *It rains*   or   *It is raining*
(b) The past tense: *It rained*   or   *It was raining*
(c) The future tense: *It will rain*   or   *It will be raining*

The form of the verb changes — we call this change *inflection* — and we can see it in the following examples:

Present tense	Past tense	Future tense
I am	I was	I shall be
you hear	you heard	you will hear
he drives	he drove	he will drive
they write	they wrote	they will write
she waits	she waited	she will wait

Sometimes a tense may indicate whether the action is *continuous* or *perfect* (which means completed):

	Present	**Past**	**Future**
CONTINUOUS	we are reading	we were reading	we shall be reading
PERFECT	they have heard	they had heard	they will have heard

The *future perfect* tense is used to show that an action *will have been* completed some time in the future:

In a year's time *I shall have taken* the O Level examination.

This tense is always used when there is an adverbial clause or phrase of time, as here — 'in a year's time'.

PARTICIPLES

The two principal parts of the verb used to form the continuous and perfect tenses are called the *present participle*, as in *reading*, and the *past participle* as in *heard*.

The present participle is used:

(a) to form the continuous tense — I am *studying*.
(b) as an adjective — a *marketing* manager
(c) in adjectival phrases — *Suffering from the heat*, he dropped out of the race.

The past participle is used:

(a) to form the past tense — They have *gone*.
(b) in adjectival phrases — The medicine, *given* to the patient in the correct doses, will aid his recovery.

Most verbs form past tenses and past participles by adding -*ed*, for example: *look, looked; wash, washed*. Some verbs form a past participle with an ending -*t* or -*en*, as in *lend, lent; beat, beaten*.

But many verbs have *irregular* past participles as well as irregular past tenses. This means that they change the basic part of the verb (also called the stem) as in *sing, sang, sung; drink, drank; drunk*.

Note
One of the commonest mistakes in writing is the use of what is called an *unrelated* present participle:

Knowing all the answers, the examination was easy for me.

The present participle should relate to the subject of the sentence. Here it appears that the examination knew all the answers, which is nonsense. The participle does not relate to the right word. The sentence should read:

Knowing all the answers, I found the examination easy.

The correct subject, *I*, now relates to the participle *knowing*.

AUXILIARY VERBS

These verbs are called *auxiliary* because they help another verb to form tenses, or indicate possibility, permission, obligation, necessity or doubt. The main auxiliary verbs are:

to be   to have   to do

Other auxiliaries frequently found are:

to dare   to need   to be able
may   must   ought   used   shall   should

Here are some examples:

I *shall* wait for you.	(auxiliary to form the future tense)
He *may* win.	(auxiliary to indicate possibility)
They *ought* to pay the bill.	(auxiliary to indicate obligation)
The minister *has* authorised it.	(auxiliary to form the perfect tense)
You *will* be sorry about this.	(auxiliary to form the future tense)

EXERCISES

1. Complete the following sentences, using the future perfect tense of the verb:

(a) They *complete* the job by six o'clock.
(b) I *not receive* the result of the examination before your departure.
(c) This firm *build* two thousand houses by the end of the year.

2. Complete the following sentences by using the continuous past tense of the verb:

(a) I *dream* about a robbery when a loud noise woke me up.
(b) While we *sing* the last verse, the organ suddenly stopped.
(c) A bomb dropped on the city just as the minister *speak* on the radio.

3. The following sentences contain an unrelated participle. Re-write the sentences correctly:

(a) Driving along Highway 7, a broken-down truck was seen blocking the way.
(b) Waiting for my friend at the bus station, a policeman came up to me.
(c) Being an oil exporting nation, OPEC admitted Venezuela as a member.

4. List the past tense and past participle of each of these verbs:

(a) seek	(d) deal	(g) swim	(j) fight
(b) rise	(e) forget	(h) wear	(k) eat
(c) choose	(f) know	(i) fall	(l) swell

5. Indicate the auxiliary verb in the following sentences:

(a) I had passed the test.
(b) He was driving the car.
(c) I have to wear glasses for reading.
(d) You must sign the form.
(e) May I see you tomorrow?
(f) He does not try hard enough.
(g) You ought to see a doctor.

6. Correct the following sentences:

(a) They digged a grave in the cemetery.
(b) Mr Harris teached us English.
(c) The building was completely destructed.
(d) The boat sinked in the storm.
(e) He falled down and broke his leg.
(f) He acts as if he is a millionaire.
(g) I explained that the car was belonging to me.

SPECIAL FORMS OF VERBS

HAVE

Sometimes the verb *to have*, when used with another verb, means 'to give effect to' or 'to cause':

BWIA *had* two aircraft withdrawn from the summer flight services to Miami.

Another use of *to have* is to express necessity or compulsion:

I *have* to start before eight o'clock in order to catch the train.

DO

The verb *to do* and its participle *done* are among the most used words in the English language. Not only is this word used as an auxiliary with other words, as in *We don't think*, but it is found in hundreds of different idioms which cannot be explained grammatically, for instance, *do with*, *do up*.

Unfortunately, this widespread use of the verb *to do* may lead to incorrect sentences like:

Crimes are *done* every day.   (*committed*)

The following general rules should be applied to the use of *to do* as a verb by itself:

(a) verbs with *-ing* used as nouns — *do* some reading
(b) *do* one's best, *do* one's duty, *do* right, *do* wrong, *do* well, *do* badly
(c) words for schoolwork — *do* lessons, *do* arithmetic, *do* exams
(d) *do* good and *do* harm
(e) *do* a favour, *do* a kindness, *do* a service
(f) *do* military service, *do* a job, etc.
(g) *do* business, *do* a trade — *doing* accountancy

MAKE

Where the verb *to do* would be wrongly used, we have to use *to make*. It is wrong to say:

I *did* an application for a job.

It is correct to say:

I *made* an application for a job.

CAN and MAY

The difference between the two words *can* and *may* is best illustrated by the questions:

Can I do this? This means — Am I able to do this?
May I do this? This means — Have I permission to do this?

Note
In the past tense *can* becomes *could* and *may* becomes *might*.

SHALL and WILL

Both these words express the future. Although they are often used interchangeably, you should know the rules for using one word in preference to the other.
Shall in the future is used for the first person singular (*I shall*) and for the first person plural (*we shall*). *Will* is used for other persons in the future.
Will is used where we wish to express strong determination, willingness or refusal:

I *will* marry Neil, whatever my parents say.

Will is also used to express command:

You *will* marry Greta. That is our final decision.

Although sometimes in modern English *will* and *shall* are both used for the first person singular and plural in the future, *shall* is still always used in questions with *I* and *we*.

Shall I go with you? Shall we all go by bus?

SHOULD and WOULD

Should is the past tense of *shall* and expresses obligation or duty:

There *should* be a national minimum wage.
You *should* take three tablets daily

Would (past tense of *will*) is used to express habitual action:

When he lived in Kingston he *would* always carry a gun.

Would is also used to express a wish or a resolve:

I *would* like to thank you for your kindness.

Should and *would* are also used to express the *conditional*, that is, something which is not certain, but which may happen, depending on certain conditions. For the first person, *I* and *we* the word *should* is used. However, people also use *would* in everyday speech. For the other persons, *you, he, she, it, they,* use *would:*

I should go to college if my parents agreed.
We should be disappointed if you did not come and see us.
He would get better if he took the medicine regularly.

58

EXERCISES

1. Re-write the following sentences, using the verb *to have* in the meaning of 'to cause':
(a) I arranged for my house to be painted.
(b) The police chief gave orders to clear the streets.
(c) She went for an eye-test.

2. Express the following sentences, using the verb *to have* in the meaning of necessity:
(a) It is necessary for me to go to the bank.
(b) The doctor was obliged to conduct a post-mortem.
(c) The company must raise $2m for expansion.

3. Begin every question with *Have you done* or *Have you made*:
(a) .... your homework yet?
(b) .... plans for your university education?
(c) .... any kind deed this week?
(d) .... any telephone calls this morning?
(e) .... any studying?

4. Write *can* or *may*, as appropriate, in the spaces:
(a) .... I be excused from attending the meeting?
(b) She .... type but her speed is rather slow.
(c) The teacher says I .... take only three subjects in the exam.
(d) I .... see you at the tennis match, but I shall not be there long.
(e) This car .... seat five passengers.

5. Rewrite these sentences, using *shall* or *will* correctly:
(a) I .... go, whatever the difficulties.
(b) They .... guard the Prime Minister's residence at the demonstration next Wednesday.
(c) .... I send it by registered post?
(d) I have tried my best with him but he .... not behave sensibly.
(e) We .... celebrate our wedding anniversary next Saturday.

6. Rewrite the following sentences, using *should* or *would* correctly:
(a) The chairman of the Parish Council said that the roads in the area were in a bad state and .... be repaired.
(b) The Senator said that he .... demand the abolition of the tax.
(c) While he was young, the parish priest .... always walk ten miles a day.
(d) The Minister said he .... welcome suggestions from us.

ADVERBS

An adverb is a word which describes a verb, an adjective or another adverb:

Eric worked *hard*. (describing a verb)
Eric is a *very* hard worker. (describing an adjective)
Eric speaks French *quite* fluently. (describing an adverb)

TYPES OF ADVERB

1. **Manner** (how)

   The pupils wrote their answers *neatly*.

2. **Time** (when)

   I *seldom* eat bananas.

3. **Place** (where)

   The disease spread *everywhere*.

4. **Degree** (how much)

   Mosquitoes are *mostly* found near swamps.

Note
Sometimes the same word may be an adjective or an adverb.

a *hard* nut (adjective)   an *early* arrival (adjective)
I work *hard*. (adverb)   He arrived *early*. (adverb).

Late is both an adjective and adverb:

The train is *late*. (adjective)
He arrived *late*. (adverb)
I shall go by a *later* train. (comparison of adjective)
He arrived *later*. (comparison of adverb)
The *latest* edition is now published. (superlative of the adjective; there is no superlative of the adverb)

ORDER OF ADVERBS

It is important to place the adverb as close as possible to the word it describes.

Adverbs of degree or time, such as:

absolutely always certainly even generally hardly
merely never often only partly quite really
seldom still

60

come in front of the verb:

I *generally* prefer   I *absolutely* agree
We *often* go   He *quite* realises

If the verb has two parts, these adverbs of degree or time come between the two parts:

I can *never* understand them.
I have *partly* forgiven him.

The most usual position for adverbs, except those listed above, is at the end of the sentence:

He pays his rent *punctually*.
The visitors greeted the President *respectfully*.

When different kinds of adverb occur in the same sentence they are arranged: 1. Degree or manner 2. Place 3. Time:

Prisoners have been *cruelly* tortured *here recently*.

COMPARISON OF ADVERBS

Refer to Lesson 10 and read once again about the comparison of adjectives. Some adverbs, like adjectives, change their form when comparisons are being used:

He will be here soon. (positive degree of adverb *soon*)
He will be here sooner than you expect. (comparative degree)
He arrived soonest of all. (superlative degree)

Most adverbs form the comparative and superlative by using *more* and *most: quickly, more quickly, most quickly*.
The following adverbs have irregular comparisons:

badly	worse	worst
far	farther	farthest
well	better	best
much	more	most
little	less	least

ALREADY, STILL, YET

These words are adverbs of time. Care must be taken in distinguishing the use of each word. They are often confused.

already means 'as early as that'; 'as late as that'; 'by that time'.
still means 'continuing now'; 'continuing then'.
yet means 'up to this time now'.

Here are some examples:

I called on him at two o'clock, but he had *already* gone.
Though he has taken many lessons he *still* cannot drive a car.
I can't pay the bill because I haven't *yet* received it.

EXERCISES

1. List the adverbs in the following sentences and say if they are adverbs of *manner, time, place* or *degree*.

(a) I always forget their names.
(b) He reluctantly agreed to my suggestion.
(c) Take this child outside.
(d) He scarcely tasted his coffee.
(e) They are usually punctual.
(f) The old man slowly climbed the steps.
(g) I do not quite understand his explanation.
(h) He went overseas with his family.
(i) The ship soon cleared the harbour.

2. List the following adverbs under the headings of **Manner, Time, Place** and **Degree**:

carefully	anywhere	weekly	nearly
under	sufficiently	truly	annually
more	immediately	everywhere	there
cheerfully	neatly	tremendously	faithfully
hungrily	too	rather	quite
tomorrow	over	rarely	below

3. In each of the following sentences the adverb has been wrongly placed. Re-write the sentences with the adverb in the right place:

(a) A large organisation in Georgetown requires a manager for its transport department urgently.
(b) Consumers of electricity have been told temporarily that the promised reduction in the price has been shelved.
(c) The president goes abroad on health grounds as well as on business regularly.
(d) Retrospectively payment was to be made from January 1st.

4. Insert the adverb *still, yet* or *already* in each of the spaces:

(a) I tried to prevent Errol from sending the letter, but he had .... sent it.
(b) Though he has been very ill he .... takes daily exercise.
(c) The result could be a draw because neither side has .... scored a goal.
(d) I advised the man to query the bill but he had .... paid it.
(e) In spite of the fact that the car is ten years old, it can .... go up a steep hill in top gear.
(f) I do not know the result of the exam because I haven't .... heard.

LESSON 15

ADVERBIAL PHRASES

As you learned in Lesson 1, a *phrase* is a group of words containing no subject or predicate. Sometimes the grammatical function of a single-word adverb can be performed by a phrase and we call this an *adverbial phrase*:

The Arawak Indians grew their crops *by traditional methods*.
Mr Prescod waited *in the airport*.
The plane leaves Freeport at *five o'clock*.

In the same way as single-word adverbs, adverbial phrases, too, are divided into the same four types, *manner, place, time* and *degree*:

with the greatest care	adverbial phrase of manner
round the corner	adverbial phrase of place
a short while ago	adverbial phrase of time
to a great extent	adverbial phrase of degree

SPECIAL FORMS OF ADVERBIAL PHRASES

There are many special forms of adverbial phrases using prepositions such as *in, on, at* and *by*. They can only be learned by use. The following are some examples:

in	*on*	*at*	*by*
in time	on purpose	at first	by all means
in sight	on time	at last	by heart
in force	on foot	at length	by surprise
in vain	on principle	at best	by oneself
in particular	on balance	at most	by accident
in advance	on trial	at least	by chance

EXERCISES

1. Write out the adverbial phrase in each sentence and say if it is one of manner, time, place or degree.

(a) The Board meets once a year.
(b) His solution was more or less correct.
(c) The car went too fast round the corner.
(d) The crowd greeted the chief with wild enthusiasm.
(e) The prevailing winds in Trinidad and Tobago blow from the north-east.
(f) I am worried about what will happen in the future.

2. Choose a suitable adverbial phrase from those listed on page 63 to fit each of the spaces in these sentences:

(a) He tried .... to open the door but it was no use.
(b) Notice .... the shape of the wings.
(c) I learned the poem ....
(d) He arrived just .... to catch the plane.
(e) You have to pay the rent ....
(f) It wasn't an accident. He did it ....
(g) .... help yourself to any drinks you like.

3. Correct these sentences. Each mistake occurs in an adverbial phrase:

(a) He can read and watch television in the same time.
(b) You will receive your certificate on due course.
(c) 'Jamaica must not be lagging for this regard,' said the President.
(d) Every then and now a face was seen at the window.
(e) He wrote an article attacking the Minister with an impunity.

4. Use a suitable adverbial phrase from the list given to fit each space in the following sentences:

through and through   under one authority
once for all   from hand to mouth
at first sight   by his own admission
without fail   in the long run

(a) He has very little money and appears to live ....
(b) .... a democracy works better than a military régime.
(c) The principal told the students .... that their behaviour must improve.
(d) Francis was a Barbadian ....
(e) The people were united ....
(f) Be at the church at three o'clock ....
(g) .... I thought the whole house was on fire.
(h) The prisoner .... is guilty of the crime.

REVISION

1. In each space put *a*, *an* or *the* as required:

(a) What is your occupation?
I am .... representative.
What is the name of .... firm employing you?
It's .... Fidelity Insurance Company.
Do you have .... bank account?
I had .... account, but it was closed.
What was the name of .... bank?
It was .... United Bank.

(b) Are you .... beautiful girl with .... charming personality and
.... right potential? .... Miss Jamaica Crown can be yours. You
have .... chance of becoming .... Queen of them all.

2. Complete the following sentences by using the correct form of
the adjective which is given on the left:

(a) ugly   She is the .... woman I have ever seen.
(b) proud   I am .... of you than I am of your brother.
(c) careless Of all the mistakes you have made that is the ....
(d) short   She was the .... of the two girls.
(e) mild   I have tried many different kinds of soap but this
              was the ....
(f) important The second item on the agenda was .... than the
              first.
(g) happy   John is always .... than Joe.

3. Express these sentences in the passive:

(a) We do not allow parking in this street.
(b) He delivered his speech in a most eloquent manner.
(c) The company provides a canteen for the benefit of the staff.
(d) You should make personal contact with the client.

4. Complete the following sentences, using the future perfect tense
of the verb:

(a) They *conclude* the meeting by three o'clock.
(b) The mechanic *not repair* your car before tomorrow.

(c) I *finish* my course at the end of year.
(d) In two more months they *harvest* the crops.

5. Give the past tense and past participle of these verbs:

(a) teach	(d) bring	(g) tear	(j) send
(b) drink	(e) eat	(h) shake	(k) know
(c) begin	(f) catch	(i) steal	(l) reply

6. Express the following sentences, using the verb *to have* with the meaning of 'to cause':
(a) I took my car for a mechanical test.
(b) The commander gave orders for the flag to be lowered.
(c) He said that he arranged for the cattle to be injected.
(d) She took her baby to the doctor for examination.

7. Use *shall* or *will* correctly in the spaces in these sentences:
(a) I .... drink what I like, in spite of what you say.
(b) They .... all vote for Mr Pierre at the next election.
(c) .... I wear a long dress for the party?
(d) He seems unable to improve his writing because he .... not listen to advice.
(e) We .... meet next time at the International Hotel.

8. Choose a suitable adverb — *still, yet* or *already* — for each space in these sentences:
(a) You can't have my exercise book because I have not .... finished my essay.
(b) I cannot connect you because the manager is .... speaking on the telephone.
(c) The man was .... dead when the ambulance arrived.
(d) Hurry up! Aren't you ready .... ?

9. Correct these sentences:
(a) He gave up smoking in the sake of his health.
(b) He told me his secret when the others were out from hearing.
(c) He travelled on the assumed name of Grant.
(d) I tell you once and all that you must stop going out with this girl.

10. List the adjectives in the following:
Buccoo Reef forms a coral garden of exquisitely delicate and intricate shapes, inhabited by swarms of countless multi-coloured tropical fish and other fascinating marine creatures.

66

LESSON 16

PREPOSITIONS

A preposition is a word which is placed before a noun or pronoun to show its relation to another word in the sentence:

The boxer hit his opponent *on* the jaw.

The preposition *on* shows the connection between *opponent* and *jaw*.

The river flows *through* the town.

The preposition *through* shows the connection between *river* and *town*.

LINKS WITH OTHER PARTS OF SPEECH

Prepositions can link a noun, pronoun or verbal noun with other parts of speech, as shown in the following examples:

Weakened *by* hunger, they surrendered to the enemy.
(adjective *weakened* linked to noun *hunger*)
He is the smartest soldier *in* the whole regiment.
(noun *soldier* linked to noun *regiment*)

Note

If a preposition is followed by a pronoun, the pronoun must be in the accusative (see Lesson 6):

Prizes have been awarded to *them* and to *me*.
To *whom* shall I give this parcel? (not to *who*)
This matter is a secret between *him* and *her*. (not *he* and *she*)

IDENTIFYING PREPOSITIONS

Many prepositions may also be used as adverbs and the two uses must be carefully distinguished. A preposition is always followed by a noun or pronoun:

He ran *down* the road. (preposition)
She looked *down*. (adverb)
He remained *behind* the door. (preposition)
He remained *behind*. (adverb)

The following is a list of the commonest prepositions:

about	behind	from	through
above	below	in	to
across	beneath	into	towards
after	beside	near	under
against	between	of	underneath
along	beyond	off	until
amid	by	on	up
among	down	over	upon
around	during	round	with
at	except	since	within
before	for	till	without

Prepositions most often express position, movement and direction. The particular use of prepositions in expressions of travel and movement needs care:

We go *from* a place to another place.
We go *by* bus, car, train, plane.
We arrive *at* the theatre.
We get *on* or *off* a train.

SPECIAL PREPOSITIONS

Like

This word can be used as a preposition and as an adjective:

He acts *like* a foreigner. (preposition)
The two boys are very *like*. (adjective)
Like most Americans, he is very self-confident. (preposition)

It is incorrect to use *like* as a conjunction in:

He speaks English *like* an Englishman does.

In the above sentence the correct word to use is *as*.

Between and among

Between should only be used when speaking of two persons or things:

Divide the cake *between* two children.

Among is used when speaking of more than two persons or things.

The prizes were distributed *among* all the winners.

Beside and besides

Beside means: 'near' or 'next to'

She sat *beside* me.

Besides means 'in addition to':

I have another car *besides* this one.

Note

Besides can be an adverb meaning 'also':

I don't like my job. *Besides*, they don't pay me very much.

In and **into**

In is used for *position*:

I have six litres of petrol *in* the tank.

Into shows *movement:*

The boy fell *into* the pool.

PREPOSITIONS WITH TIME AND DATE

Note these special uses:

at six o'clock	on Christmas day	in August 1981
at night	at Christmas	on the morning of 20th June
until midday	before Thursday	after Saturday
by six o'clock	throughout last summer	for three days

COMPOUND PREPOSITIONS

Sometimes a group of words performs the same function as a preposition. Such a group is known as a compound preposition:

because of	on account of	owing to	according to
as regards	for the sake of	in case of	in spite of
in view of	by way of		

USE OF PREPOSITIONS TO CONVEY DIFFERENT MEANINGS

It is often said that the simple preposition adds immense variety to the English language. The preposition *on*, for example, can be used in many ways. The following are a few examples:

He is *on The Tribune.* (meaning *employed by*)

The professor gave a talk *on* Caribbean writers. (meaning *about* Caribbean writers)

Have you a match *on* you? (meaning *Do you possess a match?*)

When he's sixty-five he will retire *on* a pension. (meaning *he will get a pension*)

She's *on* holiday. (meaning *away from work or school*)

He's *on* his best behaviour. (meaning *behaving as well as he possibly can.*)

EXERCISES

1. Name the prepositions in the following sentences and state the noun or pronoun which each governs:
(a) He had not a single cent on him.
(b) Thousands of spectators poured into the stadium.
(c) He could not climb over the wall.
(d) Write your date and place of birth.
(e) This company is incorporated under Bahamian law.
(f) There is a great deal of truancy among school children.

2. Use one of these prepositions to fill a space in each of the following sentences:

    before   between   without   from   across   at   beside

(a) We must leave .... eight o'clock if we have to catch the plane.
(b) I shall wake you .... seven o'clock.
(c) I sit .... my wife in church.
(d) She was so angry that she left .... saying a word.
(e) A temporary bridge was built .... the river.
(f) Joshua and his friends were stranded far .... home.
(g) My father's money was divided equally .... my sister and me.

3. Supply the correct preposition in these sentences:
(a) He is very good .... mathematics.
(b) This medicine is very good .... coughs.
(c) Save some money each week and provide .... your future.
(d) I have doubts .... your ability.
(e) The family announces .... deep regret the death of Dr Gopaul.
(f) I shall send .... a free copy of this book.
(g) A battery factory is .... construction and when completed will double the output of batteries.

4. Use one of the compound prepositions given in this lesson to fill the spaces in the following sentences:
(a) He spent all his money on gambling until he decided to give up the habit .... his children.
(b) .... warnings, many people are drowned.
(c) .... the latest published statistics of the FAO, one out of every four children in the developing world suffers from malnutrition.
(d) The coffee harvest was very low .... the drought.
(e) .... the possibility of a demonstration, the authorities have placed guards at the entrance to the university.

MORE ABOUT PREPOSITIONS

Certain prepositions must follow particular verbs or adjectives.

The following is a list of selected adjectives with the prepositions that follow them. It is not a complete list, and you should take note of others that you may come across in your reading:

accompanied by	exempt from	jealous of
accustomed to	exposed to	kind of
acquainted with	full of	notorious for
addicted to	filled with	opposite to
afraid of	free from	parallel to
agreeable to	good for	peculiar to
angry with	guilty of	prejudicial to
appropriate to	grateful for	proficient in
ashamed of	(a kindness)	proud of
dependent on	grateful to	satisfied with
different from	(a person)	similar to
disgusted at	hopeful of	superior to
(something)	identical with	surrounded by
disgusted with	ignorant of	tired of
(somebody)	incapable of	(something)
distinct from	indifferent to	tired with
eligible for	inconsistent with	(action)
envious of	innocent of	true to
equal to	intent on	worthy of
essential to	intimate with	void of

Similarly, here is a list of verbs followed by the prepositions that usually come after them:

abstain from	despair of
absolve from	deter from
accede to	die of
adapt for (a purpose)	differ with (someone)
afflict with	differ from (opinion)
agree to (a proposal)	disagree with
agree with (a person)	disapprove of
agree upon (a plan)	discourage from
aim at	excel in
allude to	exclude from

71

approve of	object to
associate with	originate in
beware of	part with (something)
blame for	part from (somebody)
boast of	prevail upon
comment on	prefer to
complain of	protect from
comply with	protest against
confide in/to	recover from
consist of	refer to
contrast with	refrain from
cope with	rely on
correspond to (a thing)	suffer from
correspond with (a person)	write to (somebody)
deprive of	write about (something)
descend from	withdraw from

PHRASAL VERBS

Many one-syllabled simple verbs in English can be combined with
particles (short, common words, mainly prepositions) to form what
are known as *phrasal verbs*. These very useful two- or three-word
combinations act as a single word with a special colloquial or
idiomatic meaning. The important and often used word *go*, for
example, can be combined with about forty particles:

go after; go against; go ahead; go along; go along
with; go at; go away; go back; go back on;
go below; go beyond; go by; go down; go down with;
go for; go forward; go in; go in for; go into; go off;
go on; go out; go over; go through; go through with;
go together; go towards; go under; go up; go with;
go without

COMPOUND WORDS FORMED WITH PREPOSITIONS

Prepositions have probably brought more new words into English
than any other part of speech. They are often combined with verbs
to form compound nouns and the following are examples of words
that have come into use in this way:

climb-down	let-up	rake-off	get-up
show-down	write-up	set-up	breakdown
build-up	hold-up	crack-down	go-between
send-off	stop-over	stand-in	fall-out

EXERCISES

1. Complete these sentences by adding the appropriate preposition to follow each verb:

(a) Gordon despaired .... passing the exam after having failed so many times.

(b) When you go out in the dark you should beware .... strangers.

(c) You should comply .... the instructions on the examination paper.

(d) The traffic jams deter many people .... taking their cars into the town.

(e) The Jamaican champion withdrew .... the feather-weight title contest.

(f) Modern architecture contrasts strikingly .... the traditional housing.

(g) The missions prevailed .... the people to build their own churches.

(h) Doctors usually advise their patients to abstain .... smoking.

(i) The Government of the Bahamas consists .... a Senate and a House of Representatives.

(j) The police inspector was deprived .... his authority.

(k) The celebrated Attila excelled .... calypso.

2. Complete these sentences by adding the appropriate preposition to follow each adjective:

(a) One of the prisoners was notorious .... his many bank robberies.

(b) This picture is different .... that one.

(c) I am disgusted .... your behaviour.

(d) He ought to be ashamed .... his untidy appearance.

(e) The tradition of carnival is peculiar .... Trinidad.

(f) Candidates for the vacancy must be proficient .... company law.

(g) The judge found him guilty .... manslaughter.

(h) Your action is worthy .... the highest praise.

(i) Young children nowadays are exposed .... many temptations.

(j) His failure in the exam is quite inconsistent .... his success in class.

(k) Make sure the wound is free .... any infection.

(l) He was quite ignorant .... the conditions of the hire-purchase.

3. Use the past tense of the verb and a preposition to make a phrasal verb in these sentences:

(a) The children were well behaved. They have evidently been well *bring.*

(b) Two minutes later a bomb *go*.
(c) He *break* in the middle of a sentence.
(d) They have *carry* extensive repairs to the road.
(e) I have not *get* the shock of my father's death.
(f) He *give* smoking when he was twenty years of age.
(g) My mother *look* eight children without any help.
(h) I borrowed a lot of money and soon *run* debt.
(i) At the university I *take* boxing and soon became heavy-weight champion.
(j) The factory in Kingston *turn* five thousand cans a day.
(k) The warning light *stand* quite clearly in the darkness.

4. The wrong preposition has been used in these sentences. Correct the sentences by supplying the right preposition:
(a) In accordance to the regulations, the road will be closed to goods vehicles.
(b) We depend of our parents during the early years.
(c) This car is superior than that.
(d) The man was accused for murder.
(e) He did his best to discourage me to doing the pools.
(f) The patient complained with a pain in the back.
(g) I prefer coffee than tea.

5. The preposition has been omitted from these sentences. Insert the correct preposition:
(a) I listen the radio every evening
(b) Because of my low income I am exempt paying taxes.
(c) The Public Library is putting a display of books by Caribbean authors.
(d) I correspond a pen-friend in England.
(e) The shareholders objected the proposal.
(f) I applied a job in an insurance office.
(g) Vincentian boat-owners have complained the poor rates paid for the transport of goods from the Eastern Caribbean.
(h) The man was very proud his son's success.
(i) I explained him how the engine worked.

6. Form compound nouns (using a hyphen where necessary) by combining a verb on the left with one of the prepositions on the right. Make as many compound nouns as you can:

verbs			prepositions		
break	turn			on	down
keep	look			out	over
set	put			in	up
sight				through	

CONJUNCTIONS

We learned in Lesson 2 that *conjunctions* are joining words. The most frequently used conjunctions are:

and but so either neither nor although
before if after that unless when while until
since because

Conjunctions link words or groups of words which are grammatical equivalents.

Adjectives: Stealing is illegal *and* immoral.
Verbs: He sang *and* danced.
Adverbs: He writes briefly *but* carefully.
Nouns: *Neither* worker *nor* employer is to blame.
Phrases: He was in great pain, *but* out of danger.
Sentences: The motorist turned back *because* the road was blocked.
He passed in English, *but* he failed in mathematics.

COMPOUND CONJUNCTIONS

There are some groups of words which have the function of conjunctions, for example:

so that   as soon as   even though   so long as

The police will not bother you *so long as* you keep out of trouble.

IDENTIFYING CONJUNCTIONS

We have noticed that some words and groups of words perform the function of other parts of speech — for instance, adverbs and adjectives. In the same way a word can sometimes act as a conjunction, adverb or preposition:

What examinations have you sat for *since* you went to the university? (conjunction)
The principal has *since* been dismissed. (adverb)
I have not seen him *since* last December. (preposition)

PAIRS OF CONJUNCTIONS

Remember that some conjunctions are used in pairs, and one must follow the other:

both .... and	neither .... nor
either .... or	not only .... but also

It is a common fault to place the first conjunction incorrectly so that the two expressions are not 'parallel', as in this example:

Fishermen on the north coast of Trinidad have either warned the government that it must settle the dispute with Venezuela or they will have to cease fishing.

This sentence should be written so that the first conjunction *either* is placed immediately in front of the first 'parallel' expression *to settle the dispute*.

Fishermen on the north coast of Trinidad have warned the government that either it must settle the dispute or they will have to cease fishing.

EXERCISES

1. Pick out the conjunctions in the following sentences:

(a) She danced all evening, although she was very tired.
(b) Since the introduction of many new mini-vans in St. Vincent, insurance companies have become alarmed at the increase in accidents.
(c) You cannot enter a university unless you have the right qualifications.
(d) The Puerto Rican lightweight champion is only twenty-one years old, whereas his opponent is ten years older.
(e) Some students seem to have plenty of money, while others can hardly afford $2 for a meal in a cafeteria.
(f) The phone will not operate unless you put a coin in first.
(g) I don't know whether it is true.

2. Join these pairs of sentences, using a conjunction:

(a) You must buy a ticket.
   If not, you cannot travel on the train.
(b) I kept my jacket on.
   It was extremely hot.
(c) I attended Harrison College.
   I went to the university.
(d) The cost of some foods increased only slightly.
   Rice even decreased.
(e) He has never held one job for more than three months.
   I don't trust him.

76

(f) We are sure of getting plenty of trade.
     We get the right stall in the market.

3. Correct these faults in the use of pairs of conjunctions:

(a) Not only is Dr Sealy an expert doctor but also a leader of the community.
(b) The chairman neither agreed to meet the deputation's demands nor to arrange for further talks.
(c) They would neither have lost their interest nor their capital.
(d) He wants both to study for an engineering diploma and a management qualification.

4. Correct the mistakes in the use or omission of conjunctions in these sentences:

(a) I shall study for the examination, even it means giving up dancing.
(b) I borrowed the money from the bank with condition that I paid it back within six months.
(c) The counter clerk at Palisadoes Airport should check the manifest so passengers booking reservations are properly dealt with.
(d) She is a good housewife except she gossips too much.
(e) He failed many times and he was not disheartened.
(f) He had neither money or position.

SOME WORDS OFTEN CONFUSED

Some words are often confused with others which have similar sounds. Others are confused because they are not used as the correct part of speech. Here is a list of some words that may cause confusion. Make sure that you know what each word means, and learn the correct pronunciation so that you can recognise differences of meaning and function.

adapt	*to change (something) so that it fits or is more suitable*
adopt	*1. to take up or follow (an argument, idea) 2. to take someone as a legal son or daughter*
accede	*to agree*
exceed	*to go beyond (a limit)*
advice	*suggestion giving help* (noun)
advise	*to make a suggestion giving help* (verb)
affect	*to change something* (verb)
effect	*result* (noun)
	to bring about (verb)
ascent	*going up* (noun)
assent	*to agree* (verb)
	agreement (noun)
adverse	*unfavourable* (adjective)
averse	*unwilling* (adjective)
abdicate	*to give up a throne*
abrogate	*to repeal (a law)*
brake	*mechanism for stopping, as in a car* (noun)
break	*to smash, destroy* (verb)
cereal	*corn or similar crops*
serial	*a story in instalments*
cite	*to quote*
sight	*the ability to see*
site	*place where something is situated*
coarse	*rough* (adjective)
course	*1. a road or track* (noun)
	2. a series of lessons (noun)

complement	*full number* (noun)
	to *complete* (verb)
compliment	*praise, flattery* (noun)
	to *praise* (verb)
contemptible	*deserving contempt or disrespect*
contemptuous	*scornful*
continual	*going on nearly all the time*
continuous	*going on all the time – without a break*
draft	*1. an order for money*
	2. a rough plan
draught	*1. a current of air*
	2. a drink
dyeing	*staining* (present participle)
dying	*ceasing to live* (present participle)
dependant	*one who depends on another* (noun)
dependent	*relying on* (adjective)
defective	*faulty*
deficient	*lacking or incomplete*
derisory	*worthy of derision or mockery*
derisive	*conveying derision or mockery*
effective	*making an effect on something/somebody*
efficient	*skilful, able to do something well*
hoard	*a hidden store*
horde	*a gang or swarm*
human	*relating to mankind*
humane	*kind, compassionate*
hanged	*past participle of hang (used for dying by hanging)*
hung	*past participle of hang (used in all other cases, e.g. a picture)*
incite	*to urge on* (verb)
insight	*the power to see into things* (noun)
loose	*not tight* (adjective)
lose	*1. to fail to keep* (verb)
	2. to be defeated (verb)
miner	*a worker in a mine* (noun)
minor	*1. less important* (adjective)
	2. a person under age (noun)
practice	*exercise work* (noun)
practise	*to perform, to exercise* (verb)

principal	1. *most important* (adjective)
	2. *a chief person* (noun)
principle	*a truth or rule* (noun)
prophecy	*a forecast* (noun)
prophesy	*to foretell* (verb)
quiet	*at rest* (adjective)
quite	*entirely* (adverb)

EXERCISES

1. Study the list above and choose a suitable word from it to fill each of the gaps in the following sentences:

(a) The company agreed with the union on the .... of the shift system.
(b) He is the .... secretary at the Ministry of Agriculture.
(c) The plant was out of action because of a .... pump.
(d) Barbados is .... in certain vital food crops.
(e) Without .... you cannot expect to become proficient.
(f) I have started to .... weight-lifting in order to strengthen my muscles.
(g) The government cannot afford to .... to the latest demands for a minimum wage.
(h) I was advised not to .... the speed limit.
(i) Political agitators sometimes .... the students to violence.
(j) The Prime Minister has great .... into the many problems of administration.
(k) The newspaper report made some .... comments on the progress of the scheme for primary education.
(l) Although he claimed to be an honest businessman he was not .... to accepting a few bribes.
(m) The shareholders thought that the dividend was .... considering how well the company was doing.
(n) There were some .... shouts from the shareholders as the chairman concluded his speech.
(o) His promotion from lecturer to senior lecturer will .... his salary.
(p) The .... of the war was widespread hunger and poverty.
(q) I must tighten this belt; it is too ....
(r) I think Australia are sure to .... against the West Indies next week.
(s) Students soon .... to the change from school to university.
(t) The efforts of the Catholic Missionaries led many people to .... the Christian faith.
(u) Few feats are as remarkable as the .... of Everest.
(v) The government will .... to the national housing programme.

80

2. After each of these sentences, a list of possible interpretations of all or part of the sentence is given. Choose which you consider the right interpretation:

(a) The regulations concerning the attendance at lectures were somewhat loose.

This means

A The regulations were immoral.
B The regulations were not strictly enforced.
C Students did not have to obey the regulations.

(b) You need business insight to make money on the stock exchange.

This means you need

A a lot of experience in business.
B a deep understanding of business.
C to have a business.

(c) Some employers would like the government to abrogate the Employees Housing Scheme.

This means

A They want the scheme removed.
B They want the scheme changed.
C They want another scheme in place of this one.

(d) After the fall in oil revenue in 1978 the construction industry quickly lost ground.

This means that construction firms

A lost a lot of estates and building sites.
B did not do as much construction work as they did before the oil price dropped.
C worked less efficiently.

(e) The police chief said he was not averse from taking strong anti-riot action in case of trouble.

The police chief meant that

A he was quite prepared to use force in case of trouble.
B he did not want to use force in case of trouble.
C he did not expect to use force in case of trouble.

(f) After three hours' discussion, the negotiations between the union and the employers broke down.

This means

A The union and the employers were unable to agree.
B The union and employers decided to meet again.
C They decided to start new negotiations.

PUNCTUATION

In speech we use pauses, different ways of expression and changes of tone to make our meaning clear. Punctuation marks help us to do the same in writing. Although there are rules about punctuation, there is room for the writer to use common sense, particularly in the use of the comma. It is very important in all writing to make sure that the meaning is conveyed correctly.

THE FULL STOP (.)

The full stop has two uses:

(a) It marks the end of a sentence.

(b) It is used after abbreviations, as in P.O. Box 1239 Mr J.O. Rodriguez, B.A.

THE COMMA(,)

The main function of the comma is to indicate a pause. It is used:

(a) to separate items in a list:

At Huggins' stores you can find radios, stereo equipment, tools, cameras and a variety of electrical goods.

However, no comma is used in the case of only two items:

We bought eggs and milk.

(b) to mark off phrases:

The President, although far from well, worked until late at night.

Commas are placed at the beginning and the end of the phrase to keep it separate from the rest of the sentence.

(c) to mark off a subordinate clause (see Lesson 22) from the rest of the sentence:

Mr Bell, who is a friend of mine, gave me an excellent testimonial.

Note

Care is needed in the use of the comma. It can alter the meaning of a sentence. Compare these sentences:

The sales manager reports the Roseau branch is doing well.
The sales manager, reports the Roseau branch, is doing well.

In the first sentence it is the sales manager who is reporting on the performance of the Roseau branch. In the second sentence it is the Roseau branch that is reporting about the performance of the sales manager.

THE SEMI-COLON(;)

The semi-colon is used to separate statements (main clauses) which could be distinct sentences but which, for reasons of style, are kept within a single sentence. The semi-colon is therefore stronger than a comma, but weaker than a full stop. The Bible makes frequent use of the semi-colon:

Idle hands make a man poor;
busy hands grow rich. (Proverbs 10)

The separate clauses which are linked by a semi-colon are usually related in meaning:

Some shareholders resent the presence of expatriates on the Board; others express gratitude for the work they have done.

THE COLON(:)

The uses of the colon are:

(a) to introduce a list:

The items on sale include: tables, chairs, cabinets, typewriters, adding machines and drawing instruments.

(b) to separate two statements in a sentence, the second of which expands the meaning of the first:

Labour unrest is a serious problem: last year there were 247 trade disputes.

THE APOSTROPHE(')

The apostrophe is used to indicate:

(a) the omission of letters:

I'll (I will)   it's (it is)   can't (cannot)

(b) possession:

the driver's licence   the students' common room (see Lesson 5 page 25)

THE HYPHEN(-)

The hyphen is used to join two (occasionally three) words into a single compound word:

swimming-pool   son-in-law   balance-of-payments

Where certain prefixes are attached to words, the hyphen follows the prefix:

pre-war   co-founder   re-write   pro-African

Numbers from twenty-one to ninety-nine also require hyphens.

THE DASH(—)

This introduces a break in the sentence where the writer wishes to say something which represents a change of thought:

At the same time packing cases full of machinery —some of them on the rubbish tip — were found to contain millions of dollars worth of equipment.

THE QUESTION MARK(?)

A question mark is used at the end of a question:

Where have you been? Did you see the film at the Plaza?

When a question is *indirect*, however, the question mark must not be used:

I asked him where he had been.
I asked him if he had seen the film at the Plaza.

THE EXCLAMATION MARK(!)

This is used to express sudden emotion or surprise. Sometimes it is used to emphasise an order:

Help!   Splendid!   Stop that at once!

QUOTATION MARKS (" .... ") (' .... ')

Quotation marks are sometimes called *inverted commas* and it is considered correct also to use single inverted commas. They enclose *direct speech*, that is, the actual words or thoughts of a speaker:

Mr Williams said, 'Please give as much as you can.'

Quotation marks are also used for names of special importance, such as titles of books, etc.:

The Guyanese author, E.R. Braithwaite, wrote the best-selling book, 'To Sir with Love'.

PARENTHESES or BRACKETS ( )

The function of brackets is similar to that of dashes. Words enclosed in brackets do not belong to the main part of the sentence, which should remain grammatically correct even if the bracketed words were removed. The words in brackets are usually a kind of after-thought or extra explanation:

Large numbers of Frenchmen (exiles from the Revolution) settled along the coast of Trinidad.

84

EXERCISES

1. Insert commas in these sentences where necessary:

(a) Haitians descendants of African slaves brought to the country by the French in the seventeenth century are generally super-stitious believe in voodoo (witchcraft) and thought Papa Doc had supernatural powers.

(b) If you would like an ideal holiday in the Bahamas why not try the Ambassador Hotel the Cable Beach Hotel the Paradise Grand Hotel or the Nassau Beach Hotel?

(c) Though he was ill for the last five years of his life the artist completed a large number of pictures.

2. Punctuate the following:

(a) Im sure Ive failed the geography examination said Greta what makes you think that asked Mother because I could answer only two questions Greta replied.

(b) Under Clive Lloyd the longest serving captain the West Indies cricket team has been all conquering their record crowns a ninety-year struggle against tremendous world opposition but if a united West Indies can face the world in cricket why not in football or athletics.

(c) The shortage of water in some parts of the country which affects industrial production could be overcome by the construction of a new reservoir.

(d) The girls mother complained that she had been refused admission to the childrens hospital.

3. Although the full stops between the letters of abbreviations are now tending to disappear, some full stops are still retained. What do the following letters and groups of letters mean?

BWIA	OPEC	Lt.	OECS
M.A.	ALCOA	OAU	P.T.O.
USA	R.S.V.P.	a.m.	UNO
AGM	CARICOM	B.C.	p.m.
Ph.D.	B.Sc.	i.e.	USSR

4. By combining one word from box A with one word from box B make compound words, using a hyphen in each case:

A			B		
take	anti		based	nail
eye	wind		skinned	century
trade	oil		control	glass
drawing	cross		away	board
thick	finger		chairman	choice
looking	multiple		tunnel	catching
nineteenth	well		reference	mark
vice	pest		communist	being

LESSON 21

CAPITAL LETTERS

We learned in Lesson 1 that a sentence must begin with a capital letter. We learned in Lesson 4 that a proper noun should also begin with a capital letter.

In addition capital letters must be used:

(a) for all national adjectives — French, German, Nigerian, etc.
(b) for the pronoun *I*.
(c) at the beginning of direct or quoted speech:

The policeman asked me, 'Why are you parking your car here?'

(d) for the days of the week and the months of the year.

Study this letter, noting all the capital letters and where they occur:

> *34 Spooners Hill,*
> *St Michael.*
>
> *28th November 198-*
>
> *The Editor,*
> *Barbados Advocate,*
> *P.O. Box 230,*
> *Bridgetown.*
>
> *Dear Sir,*
>   *I am sure all Barbadians will support the move to provide beach kiosks and sales booths to prevent unlicensed selling and harassment of tourists on our beautiful beaches. After all, tourists are our main source of revenue and every effort must be made to reverse the recent decline in this industry which provides employment for more than 10,000 people.*
>
> *Yours truly,*
> *Patricia Harrison*

EXERCISES

1. Write out the following sentences correctly, using capital letters where necessary:

(a) mr miller teaches at a training college. he is a mathematics teacher.

(b) mrs garcia works in a local hospital. she is a nurse
(c) the meeting was addressed by ulf senator sahadoo. he is a politician.
(d) joe goes to a special school. he is blind.
(e) deputy prime minister of antigua and barbuda, lester bird has criticised britain's reduced aid to the caribbean.
(f) not many british people speak japanese, but japan exports a great deal to britain.
(g) bwia flies from heathrow direct to trinidad, with connections to caracas, grenada, st lucia, st vincent, antigua and other caribbean islands.

2. Put the capital letters in the following passages:

(a) when the british explorer clapperton had audience with sultan bello he found the latter reading euclid in arabic and he then entered into a discussion with the sultan on the merits of christianity. these rulers in hausaland were scholars and statesmen, educated on an islamic system of training which was centuries old.

(b) notice is hereby given that the twenty-second annual general meeting of the company will be held at the conference centre, grand bahama, on wednesday november 13th 1985 at 11 a.m.

(c) the third annual meeting of the general assembly of the caribbean reinsurance corporation began in georgetown, guyana on tuesday last week. the jamaican delegation was led by the permanent secretary, ministry of finance.

(d) i am grateful to the holy ghost fathers, and to the fathers of the society of african missions for their valuable help. i would also like to record my thanks to the british museum and to the bodleian library, oxford.

(e) producer akie dean began by promoting african bands like the afro-nationals and super combo from sierra leone, the african brothers from ghana and the funkees from nigeria, the first entry in the british hit parade came in january 1980 when 'i love you for ever' reached number five in the disco charts. this was followed by another african disco chart buster,' weakness for your sweetness' by jimmy senyah from barbados.

(f) the west indies, jubilant over their test drubbing of australia in perth, arrived in sydney yesterday with the captain clive lloyd declaring, 'we haven't had enough match practice. we are still patchy.'

THE CLAUSE

A *clause* is a group of words forming part of a sentence and containing a subject and a predicate. It must therefore be distinguished from a phrase, which has neither subject nor predicate:

> As Pedro sat in his hut that night, gazing into a log fire, he thought over the matter.

The sentence above contains one phrase and two clauses:

> *phrase* gazing into a log fire.
> *clause* (a) as Pedro sat in his hut (subordinate)
> (b) he thought over the matter (main)

MAIN and SUBORDINATE CLAUSES

A main clause can stand alone, since it expresses a complete thought. It is sometimes referred to as an independent clause. In the above example *he thought over the matter* is a main clause.

A subordinate, or dependent, clause does not express a complete thought, but gives more information about another part of the sentence. In the above example *As Pedro sat in his hut* tells us more about the verb *thought*. It explains what Pedro was doing *when* he thought the matter over.

TYPES OF CLAUSE

1. Adjectival clause

This does the work of an adjective in describing a noun or pronoun in the main clause. It usually begins with a relative pronoun *who, which, that, whose,* and *whom*:

> The author Michael Anthony, *who was born in Mayaro*, began his writing career in 1951.

Sometimes the relative pronoun is omitted, but its function is understood:

> Where is the chisel *I left on the bench*?

In the above example the relative pronoun *which* is understood after *chisel*.

2. Adverbial clause

This does the work of an adverb by telling us more about the verb in the main clause. It is often introduced by such words as *when,*

88

where, as, after, although, while, unless, because, before, until:

The match had ended in a draw at full time *before the referee awarded penalty-kicks* to decide the result.

Adverbial clauses can be recognised by the work they do in adding information to the main verb. They can be listed as follows:

(a) *Time, place and manner*

When Mr Joseph was in Arima, he bought a number of presents for his wife. (time)

(b) *Reason and purpose*

The doctor gave the patient an anti-tetanus injection *because he thought the wound was infected.* (reason)

The invigilator sits in the examination room *so that no one is able to cheat.* (purpose)

(c) *Concession*

Sometimes a sentence contains a subordinate clause which 'concedes' a contrary point. The most usual introductory word is *although*:

Although he had a very poor education, he managed to reach a high position in the firm.

(d) *Result*

The words *so* and *such,* followed later in the sentence by *that,* express a result:

The price of most foodstuffs is *so* high *that housewives are now forced to economise.*

(e) *Condition*

Conditions are expressed by words such as *if* and *provided:*

Have you decided what you will do *if you do not pass the examination?*

You might get a job in the Ministry of Agriculture, *provided you have the right qualifications.*

3. Noun clause

A noun clause does the work of a noun:

How much the managing director is paid is no business of mine.

The subordinate clause in the above sentence has the function of a noun and is the subject of the sentence.

Note

Remember that it is important to place the subordinate clause *as close as possible* to the noun, verb or adjective it qualifies. Failure to do this can make the meaning unclear. For example:

In South Africa many students held protest meetings on the university campus where the apartheid laws are still in force.

What the writer meant was that the apartheid laws are still in force in South Africa. The sentence should read:

In South Africa, where the apartheid laws are still in force, many students held protest meetings on the university campus.

Here is a similar example:

Manufactured goods are a serious threat to honest traders if they are smuggled into the country.

This should read:

Manufactured goods, if they are smuggled into the country, are a serious threat to honest traders.

EXERCISES

1. Write out the subordinate clauses in the following sentences and in brackets identify the type of clause — *noun, adjectival* or *adverbial*.

(a) The committee congratulates the chairman who has today reached the age of seventy.

(b) He has saved regularly from his salary so that he will be able to pay for a good education for his children.

(c) People want to know how Guyana has progressed in the past year.

(d) The new mosquito destroyer is a safe and effective appliance because it kills all insects without smoke or burning.

(e) The scenery was so beautiful that it took my breath away.

(f) Bahamas Electricity Corporation invites applications from suitably qualified and experienced persons who seek a management career in the company's Public Relations Department.

(g) The policeman noticed that the car had two flat tyres.

(h) Leave a message on the manager's desk where it can be easily seen.

(i) Will you please help me to trace my friend James Clark who was at the Government High School, in 1974.

2. Write out the subordinate adverbial clauses in the following sentences and in brackets identify the type of adverbial clause — *time, place, manner, reason, purpose, concession, result* or *condition*.

(a) Although Mr Singh had a weak back, he still managed to cultivate his small farm.

(b) I am not taking mathematics in the examination as I find it rather boring.
(c) It was such a hot day that nobody wanted to work hard.
(d) When Joseph was eating his meal, his wife was cleaning the room.
(e) You will have to wait three hours if you miss the plane.
(f) The next day there was a terrible storm, exactly as the weather forecast had predicted.
(g) Don't park the car where I shall not be able to find it.

3. Combine each pair of sentences into a single sentence containing a subordinate clause:

(a) Burglars entered his house, taking all his valuables.
He was away on holiday.
(b) The bauxite industry is highly mechanised.
For this reason it employs only about 6000 persons on a full-time basis.
(c) Parents of pupils at schools in the Hawksbill area have written to the Ministry of Education.
They complained of air pollution from nearby factories.
(d) Not wishing to act against his wishes, I shall not go.
He gives his consent.
(e) She will certainly die.
She does not see a doctor.
(f) A group of students at the university campus carried placards.
The placards demanded that the educational cuts be restored.
(g) The truth is that our programme is unlikely to succeed.
We have now realised the truth.

4. Rewrite the following sentences so that the subordinate clause or phrase is correctly placed or altered to avoid ambiguity or absurdity:

(a) A little girl has been found by a policeman who was wearing a white frock.
(b) I am a qualified accountant with experience in supervising office work and cleaning women.
(c) Most boys love watching a football match, who have played football at school.
(d) If the baby does not thrive on fresh milk, it should be boiled.
(e) Slaves were exported from Nigeria and did not cease until the naval blockade in the late 1830s, long after the British prohibited the slave trade in 1807.

DIRECT AND INDIRECT SPEECH

DIRECT SPEECH

This is the term used when we write the exact words of the speaker. These words are usually preceded by a comma and put inside inverted commas:

> The Minister said, 'I urge you to consider ways of developing trade.'

INDIRECT SPEECH

This form of speech gives the words of the speaker as reported by someone else. It is also known as *reported speech*, and is usually introduced by a verb of *saying* in the past tense. Newspapers use indirect speech when reporting what government ministers and other important people have said at public meetings:

> The Minister *said* that cocoa production was rising.
> The minister *urged* them to consider ways of developing trade.

CHANGING DIRECT TO INDIRECT SPEECH

There are rules to be followed when changing direct to indirect speech:

(a) First and second person pronouns (*I, we, you*) become third persons pronouns (*he, she, they*).

(b) The present tense becomes the past tense:

has	becomes	*had*
are	becomes	*were*
shall	becomes	*should*
may	becomes	*might*

(c) Words denoting nearness in time and place become words denoting distance or remoteness:

now	becomes	*then*
this	becomes	*that*
today	becomes	*that day*
yesterday	becomes	*the day before*

(d) It may be necessary to add a noun in brackets to make clear the meaning conveyed in the direct speech:

> Ali said to his friend, 'You have taken the wrong turning.'
> Ali told his friend that he (his friend) had taken the wrong turning.

(e) The clause containing the verb of *saying* in the past tense sometimes indicates what kind of statement was made. Verbs such as *urged, replied, ordered, declared, demanded, enquired, advised, suggested* are often used:

> 'Try a little harder,' said the professor. (direct)
> The professor *urged* him to try a little harder. (indirect)

> 'Why is there no bus to Kingstown on this route?' he asked. (direct)
> He *enquired* why there was no bus to Kingstown on that route. (indirect)

> The speaker said, 'Some Caribbean islands are doubling their population within a few years and this is hardly a matter for us to be complacent about.' (direct)
> The speaker said that some Caribbean islands were doubling their population within a few years and this was hardly a matter for them to be complacent about. (indirect)

SPEECH WORDS

The following list is a selection of words which are more expressive than *say*. They are not a complete list and you should make a list of additional words you notice in the course of your reading:

Refusal contradict refuse deny forbid refute
Command command dictate direct insist order
Request ask beg entreat plead request
Agreement agree confirm assent admit
Distress cry groan
Argument protest reason state urge confess argue

Note
While the word *say* can be used in both direct and indirect speech, the chief use of *tell* is in indirect speech only. Similarly, care must be exercised in the use of some other speech words. We would not, for example, use the word *groan* in direct speech, but it is quite correct to use it at the end of a direct quotation:

> 'I think my leg is broken,' she groaned.

EXERCISES

1. Rewrite the following sentences in indirect speech:

(a) He said, 'If you have more mobile police on the roads it will probably reduce the number of accidents.'

(b) 'Do you drive every day to Bridgetown, Joe, or do you take the bus?' I enquired.

(c) 'I want you to finish your English test today,' said Mr Neal to Elizabeth.

(d) 'I'll bring the book back tomorrow,' she promised.

(e) 'I didn't scratch your car,' the truck driver said to the owner of the Mercedes.

(f) I asked the carpenter, 'Will you please replace the handles before hanging the doors.'

(g) Mr Foster said, 'This is the only way by which clashes with the police can be avoided.'

(h) 'Don't worry, I'll take good care of your car,' the attendant assured me.

(i) 'I really think chili con carne is the best dish on the menu today,' the waiter said to us.

(j) Before leaving, my father said to me, 'Keep an open mind, listen to advice and don't be too proud to take it.'

2. Rewrite the following sentences in direct speech:

(a) I demanded to know what right he had to examine my licence, since I had no proof of his authority.

(b) She told him not to worry and that she would clean the house thoroughly.

(c) One of the bank managers said that he was going to stop issuing travellers' cheques to anyone he didn't know.

(d) The Minister of Agriculture declared that farming had become unattractive and unproductive and only a sustained new policy would solve the problem.

(e) He reminded us that we had not paid our bill.

(f) She asked him if he went there often.

(g) He said that he believed many of the signatures on the document were forged.

(h) He refused to pay the bill unless the manager would agree to reduce the amount.

(i) He suggested that we went to a night club without him.

PREFIXES AND SUFFIXES

The main part of a word is called its *root*. We can add to the root, to make new words. The parts we add are called *prefixes* if they are joined to the front of the root, and *suffixes* if they are added after the root. They may consist of only one letter, or one or two syllables. Here are some examples:

root port + *prefix* im = *new word* import
root deep + *suffix* ly = *new word* deeply

PREFIXES

It is useful to be able to recognise some of the commonest prefixes. The list below sets out some of them, and if you remember their meanings they will help you in vocabulary studies and in understanding new words.

inter:	between	post:	after
re:	again, back	pre:	before
un:	not	sub:	under
ad:	to	trans:	across
super:	over	tri:	three
bene:	good	semi:	half
bi:	twice	mono:	single
co:	together	micro:	very small
ex:	out of	mega:	very large
mis:	wrongly	tele:	far away
proto:	first	auto:	self
poly:	many	anti:	against
multi:	many	ante:	before

Here are some words using these prefixes:

prototype	the first model of a new machine
transparent	able to be seen through
beneficial	able to do good
polygamy	having several wives
autobiography	a person's life story written by himself
microfilm	photographic film for small scale reproduction of documents
antecedent	something that comes before
misuse	the wrong use
supernumerary	a person who is additional to the usual number

Sometimes a hyphen is added when a prefix is joined to a word, but the rule is to use the hyphen only to make the meaning clear. For example, we would write *recover*, meaning to 'get back' something that had been lost, but if we write *re-cover* we mean 'to cover again'. We also use a hyphen to avoid having an awkward double vowel, as in *re-establish, re-adjust* and *co-operate*.

One of the commonest uses of a prefix is to give the opposite meaning to that of the root word. Such prefixes are *ab, de, dis, ig, il, im, in, ir, non, un, extra*. You will find, however, that not every word beginning with *dis* or *mis* or *re* necessarily comes from a root word with a prefix added. For example, *discuss, miserable* and *regard* have not been formed in this way.

SUFFIXES

Here again, it is helpful to know some of the suffixes most frequently found. They are:

ary	ate	ics	ible	ness
ery	ly	ology	able	hood
er	ent	scope	graph	ship
al	ant	en	ine	ling
ory	tion	ify	ism	ment

You find these in words such as:

bravery	innate	geology	readable	sickness
final	action	purify	realism	movement

The suffix *ive* means 'having the nature or quality of'. This suffix is often used to change a word to another part of speech. Sometimes there is a change in the ending of the root form before the suffix is added:

represent (verb)	*representative* (noun)
sense (noun	*sensitive* (adjective)
conserve (verb)	*conservative* (adjective)

Adding the suffix *ic* to a noun changes the noun to an adjective:

enthusiast (noun)	*enthusiastic* (adjective)
egotist (noun)	*egotistic* (adjective)

The suffix *ity* means condition, state, quality or degree:

secure (adjective)	*security* (noun)
personal (adjective)	*personality* (noun)
public (adjective)	*publicity* (noun)

The suffix *ness* means condition, state, quality or degree and it changes an adjective to an abstract noun:

kind (adjective)	*kindness* (noun)
mad (adjective)	*madness* (noun)

The suffix *eer* is a noun suffix used for people who do some particular job or are concerned with an act:

auction (noun)	*auctioneer* (noun)
engine (noun)	*engineer* (noun)

The usual form for indicating a branch of science is made by adding the suffix *ics*:

physics optics mechanics mathematics electronics genetics

The suffix *(o)logy* usually indicates a branch of knowledge, which could also be a science:

anthropology archaeology biology psychology technology ecology

EXERCISES

1. Here are some words with the prefix *dis* —

    disallow discourage discard discount disparage discourse discontent disapprove discredit disgrace

    State which word you would use:

    (a) to make people doubt something
    (b) to throw out or reject
    (c) not to approve
    (d) for describing a state of not being satisfied
    (e) not to encourage
    (f) to say something that is bad
    (g) to refuse to accept
    (h) for a percentage less than the normal price
    (i) for shame
    (j) for a talk or conversation

2. Add the appropriate suffix, *ary, ery* or *ory*, to the following:

(a) surg –	(e) diction –	(i) annivers –
(b) mission –	(f) dilat –	(j) tempor –
(c) compuls –	(g) cemet –	(k) honor –
(d) volunt –	(h) direct –	(l) embroid –

3. Add a prefix to the following words to give the opposite in meaning:

(a) human	(b) perfect	(c) true	(d) normal
(e) audible	(f) noble	(g) clockwise	(h) sense

4. In each of the following sentences write the complete word where the suffix has been omitted:

(a) It is the government's intention to *modern* – the water supply.
(b) The army must *strength* – its defences.
(c) In my medical course at the university I have to study *pathol* –.
(d) The Jamaica police have started a *vigor* – offensive against criminals in the country.
(e) The medicine will certainly have a *benefic* – effect.
(f) These types give *versat* – service on all roads, surfaced or unsurfaced.
(g) The jetty was developed to reduce *congest* – at the port.
(h) A wages explosion would seriously damage the Guyanese *monet* – policy.
(i) The doctor examined the patient's chest with a *stetho* –.
(j) An early Picasso painting is now quite *price* –.
(k) Linden, sixty-seven miles from Georgetown, is *access* – by ocean-going vessels.

5. Complete these words and word roots by adding *able* or *ible*:

(a) forc –
(b) agree
(c) aud –
(d) change
(e) comfort
(f) consider
(g) convert
(h) drink
(i) elig –
(j) inevit –
(k) irresist –
(l) poss –
(m) reason
(n) regrett –
(o) respons –
(p) valu –
(q) unthink –
(r) neglig –
(s) corrupt
(t) flex –

6. What numbers are represented in each of the following words? Use your dictionary to help you:

(a) centipede (b) sextet (c) octagon (d) tripod
(e) quadruped (f) monogamy (g) bifocal (h) kilometre

7. Find words corresponding to each of the definitions given below, starting with one of the following prefixes:

geo peri poly syn mono trans super pre

(a) false reason
(b) to happen at the same time
(c) word of one syllable
(d) science of the earth's crust
(e) edge
(f) figure with five or more sides
(g) to change from one language to another
(h) cannot be explained by physical laws

REVISION

1. Supply the correct preposition in each of these sentences:

(a) I am ashamed .... my failure in the examination.
(b) She takes great pride .... her appearance.
(c) I apologise .... my clumsiness.
(d) Everybody was provided .... a dictionary.
(e) The defendant protested .... the large fine imposed on him.
(f) Some English words are derived .... Latin.
(g) The two boys are so much alike, I cannot distinguish .... them.
(h) I congratulate you .... passing your examination.

2. Use the past tense of the verb and a preposition to make a phrasal verb in each of these sentences:

(a) In his speech the principal *hint* the need for harder work.
(b) After several attempts I *give* all hope of getting into a university.
(c) He *pay* his debts promptly.
(d) Before they left the house they *dispose* all the furniture.
(e) He does not eat meat. For years he *live* fruit and nuts.
(f) This shop *come* new management last week.
(g) The shop-keeper *wrap* the parcel.
(h) I *agree* what the last speaker said.

3. Join each pair of sentences, using a conjunction:

(a) I was ill.
    I managed to crawl to the telephone.
(b) I asked the clerk why the plane was delayed.
    He did not reply.
(c) Because of her injuries she could not dance.
    She could not swim.
(d) We shall be able to have a good holiday next year.
    We can save enough money.
(e) The students put down their pens.
    The teacher told them to stop writing.

4. Punctuate, putting in capital letters where necessary:

(a) He said Im going to sell this car and buy a new one how much do you want for it asked kenny about $3000 answered joe.

(b) Notice is hereby given that the register of members and transfer books will be closed from 20th to 27th July 1982 both dates inclusive for the purpose of paying the final dividend and bonus issue by order of the board.

5. Combine each pair of sentences into a single sentence containing a subordinate clause:
(a) Candidates for this post must have a qualification in accountancy. They should be able to communicate with senior management.
(b) The manager was suddenly taken ill.
He was interviewing a customer.
(c) I hope to arrive in time for dinner.
Of course, the plane may be late.
(d) The news of the robbery was telephoned to the police station. Immediately afterwards a suspect was arrested.

6. Rewrite the following in indirect speech:
(a) The chairman remarked, 'All this is out of order; it is beside the point, and you have wasted the committee's time.'
(b) The teacher asked him, 'Do you want to go to a university to study for a veterinary degree or would you prefer to follow a career in medicine?'

7. Rewrite the following in direct speech:
(a) The doctor asked if he had eaten anything that day.
(b) The policeman said that the accident was entirely due to the boy's own fault, and that he had not stopped before he crossed the road.

8. Add a prefix to give the opposite meaning:
(a) flexible   (b) modest   (c) belief   (d) secure
(e) courteous   (f) familiar   (g) respectful (h) normal

9. Write the complete word where the suffix has been omitted:
(a) He made a great *improve* – to his house.
(b) *Prevent* – measures were taken in case of any disturbance.
(c) This pesticide will *elim* – all insects in the house.
(d) The general was wearing a *decorat* – on his uniform.
(e) There was an *end* – stream of traffic on the road to Arima.
(f) The *electric* – repaired the fuse.
(g) The *ten* – had not paid the rent.

LESSON 25

SPELLING

Incorrect spelling creates a poor impression, and it can cause you to lose many marks in your examinations. English is a language with many rules, oddities and exceptions in its spelling. The one sure way to become proficient in spelling is to read widely, so that you constantly meet words in print and get to know them. The regular use of a good dictionary will help you to check not only spelling, but also meaning and pronunciation.

Sometimes errors are caused by confusion between words that sound alike, as with *practice* (noun) and *practise* (verb), or words that look rather similar, as with *deprecate* and *depreciate*.

The rules which follow are only a general guide, but most of the worst pitfalls of spelling — words like *accommodate* — have to be learned by heart, in the form of a mental drill:

accommodate has *double c* and *double m*

or the little rhyme:

i before *e*, except after *c*

which is explained in Rule 1 below.

RULES

1. When *ei* or *ie* has the sound *ee* (as in *feel*), the *i* comes before the *e* except when it follows *c*:

   grief piece ceiling receive *exception:* seize

2. Adding a suffix beginning with a vowel (-*ing* -*er* -*ed*)

(a) If the word consists of one syllable ending in a vowel and a consonant, the consonant is usually doubled:

   beg, beggar; stop, stopping; rag, ragged

(b) In a word of more than one syllable, ending in a vowel and a consonant, the final consonant is doubled if the last syllable is stressed:

   forbid, forbidden; occur, occurred; begin, beginning

(c) In a word of more than one syllable, ending in a vowel and a consonant, the final consonant is *not* doubled if the last syllable is unstressed:

   suffer, suffered; limit, limited; offer, offering

(d) Words ending in a single vowel followed by *l* usually double the final *l*, whether the last syllable is stressed or not:

> travel, traveller; cancel; cancellation

However, there are exceptions, such as *parallel, paralleled.*

3. Words ending in a consonant followed by *e*
(a) Usually the *e* is dropped when a suffix beginning with a vowel is added:

> come, coming; move, movable; dine, dining

(b) The *e* is usually kept after *g* or *c* to show that the pronunciation of these consonants is soft:

> manage, manageable; advantage, advantageous; notice, noticeable.

4. The prefix *dis* follows a logical pattern. If the first letter of the word to which the prefix is added is *s* then a *double s* will occur. In other cases there will be a *single s*:

> disappear, dissatisfy, dissimilar, disable

5. The *u* is kept in adjectives ending in *able*, but not in adjectives ending in *ous*, where the noun ending is *our:*

> honour, honourable; favour, favourable; glamour, glamorous; humour, humorous; odour, odorous; rigour, rigorous.

6. Plural of words ending in *y*. You will find them also in Lesson 5. If the letter before *y* is a vowel add *s*:

> valley, valleys; day, days

If the letter before *y* is a consonant, change the *y* to *i* and add *es*:

> baby, babies; remedy, remedies

SIGNPOSTS

While the following 'signposts' cannot be considered rules, they will help to alert you to some of the pitfalls in spelling. Watch for:

eous and **ious**

> furious   serious   cautious   envious   previous   curious
> courteous   outrageous   gorgeous   courageous

er and **or**

> employer   lawyer   caterer   hairdresser   surveyor   curator
> solicitor   professor

102

ant and **ent**

 vacant   indignant   pleasant   inhabitant   ignorant   intelligent
 impudent   independent   obedient

ei

 foreign   weight   eighty   heir   height   vein   reign

sion and **tion**

 pension   decision   occasion   addition   calculation

ui

 suitable   recruit   nuisance   bruise   juice

silent w

 wrap   wretch   sword   wreck   write   wrong   wreath

ea (sounding e and ee)

 neat   teacher   deal
 health   weather   pleasure

al   el   il   le

 loyal   travel   peril   bottle

able and **ible**

 reasonable   visible   valuable   flexible

ful

 handful   plateful   sackful   gleeful   remorseful

SOME WORDS COMMONLY MISSPELT

The following list is grouped so that you can practise ten a day.
Memorise each group, and then write out those words without looking at the book.

(a)	(b)	(c)	(d)
absence	committee	advertisement	maintenance
definite	comparative	believe	usually
acquire	seize	consensus	omitted
disappear	separate	valuable	recommend
business	exaggerate	parallel	occasion
category	humour	imaginary	persuade
necessary	immediately	dissolve	similarly
conscious	independent	despair	embarrass
criticise	decision	development	miscellaneous
legible	supersede	privilege	difference

103

(e)	(f)	(g)	(h)
accommodate	itinerary	grievance	equipped
straight	scenery	permissible	emphasise
receive	column	procedure	sergeant
laboratory	exercise	view	noticeable
conscientious	convenience	government	occurred
humorous	appropriate	expenses	permanent
anxious	exhausted	competitive	proprietary
precious	transferred	courtesy	foreign
efficient	prejudiced	hypocrisy	surgeon
possess	influential	essential	skilful

(i)	(j)
extinguish	descend
acquaintance	association
vehicle	acknowledge
medicine	leisure
inflammable	discipline
excitement	agreeable
combustible	suppression
glamorous	elementary
eccentric	mechanical
undoubtedly	desperate

EXERCISES

1. Using the rules given in this lesson, complete the missing words in each of the following sentences:

(a) Kingston is the ch—f town of Jamaica.
(b) He dec—ved me by not keeping his promise.
(c) Last Tuesday was the ho—est day of the year.
(d) The school roll is limi—ed to 350.
(e) I was rac—g to catch the bus when I fell.
(f) He made me an advantag—s offer for my car.

2. Follow these patterns to make other words from those given in italics:

(a) plenty, plentiful, plentifully
    duty fancy mercy pity beauty

(b) faith, faithful, faithfully
    law thought doubt success wrong

(c) try, tried, trying
    cry dry empty remedy pacify

3. What are the present participles (-ing) of these verbs?

(a) appeal	(e) imitate	(i) apologise	(m) stop
(b) compel	(f) verify	(j) rebel	(n) deplore
(c) travel	(g) announce	(k) explode	(o) die
(d) eliminate	(h) challenge	(l) care	(p) issue

4. From the list of commonly misspelt words write the words which mean:

Group (a)

obtain, classification, comment unfavourably, not being there, aware

Group (b)

straight away, make things seem larger, take the place of, official group of people, making up your mind

Group (c)

generally agreed opinion, make solid into liquid, favour, hopelessness, worth a lot of money

Group (d)

make someone feel uncomfortable, left out, varied, advise someone to do something, keeping/upkeep

Group (e)

funny, provide a lodging for someone, very worried, own, not curved

Group (f)

feeling against someone, moved to another place, route, suitable, worn out/finished

Group (g)

money spent, grounds for complaint, politeness, can be allowed, necessary

Group (h)

stress the importance, happened, clever, easily seen, supplied with

Group (i)

easily catches fire (*two different words*), odd, put out (a fire), person you know, attractive/enchanting

Group (j)

free time, keeping people under control, basic/simple, group/society, go down.

LESSON 26

PHRASAL VERBS

You have already met *phrasal verbs* briefly in Lesson 16. They are combinations of verbs and certain particles (prepositions or adverbs) which can have many shades of meaning. A complete mastery of all the meanings of phrasal verbs in English can only be achieved by wide reading and experience in the use of everyday colloquial speech.

The simplest use of particles with verbs is when the particles express direction. The particles commonly used with verbs of motion in this sense are:

> in　out　down　off　on　away　over　around　about
> 　　through　back　along　across　past　by

The verb *get* illustrates the variety of phrasal verbs that may be made in this way:

> I *got in* the bus
> I *got off* the train
> What time did you *get back*?
> The old lady *got up* the stairs.
> The water *gets through* the roof.
> The robbers managed to *get past* the security guards.
> The truck was in the way but I *got round* it
> The burglar *got over* the fence
> I *got away* from school early.

These examples are easy to understand, but many phrasal verbs have an idiomatic meaning, which is different from the usual meaning of the separate words that make up the phrasal verb:

> I haven't *got over* my illness.
> How is Sally *getting on* at school?
> You will have to *get round* to working faster.

The following are some phrasal verbs using *bring:*

bring up	children/a subject in conversation
bring off	a deal
bring on	a cold
bring in	a new idea
bring over	(convert to a new idea)
bring down	prices/a government
bring about	cause to happen
bring forward	(move to an earlier date)

106

Similarly, the verb *break* when used with different particles takes on a special meaning:

break down	a car
break in	a house
break off	negotiations
break out	war
break up	a fight
break away	(separate)

Some phrasal verbs contain two particles:

break out in	spots
look out for	someone/something
team up with	(make a partnership)
do away with	(get rid of)
go through with	(continue to the end)
check up on	(get details about)
send out for	(have somebody fetch)
stand in for	(replace someone)
put up with	(bear)
go on with	(continue)
hit back at	(attack one's attacker)
look in on	(visit someone)

In the idiomatic meaning a preposition sometimes changes its original sense. For instance, the preposition *with* normally implies 'accompaniment', but in *A miser hates to part with his money* and *I can dispense with my jacket* it implies 'separation'. Similarly, in the sentence *The two men fell out with each other* it implies separation or disagreement.

In the more recent and colloquial expression *Get with it* the sense returns to 'accompaniment'.

EXERCISES

1. Complete the phrasal verb in each of the following sentences:

(a) The crowd was carried .... by the Minister's speech.
(b) They are now carrying .... extensive repairs on the expressway.
(c) The eldest son will carry .... the business when Mr Rodriguez dies.
(d) Alex Donald carried .... the tennis title again.
(e) The President called .... his advisers for an urgent meeting.
(f) The union called .... its threatened strike at the bauxite plant.
(g) The manager called .... a report on the sales campaign.
(h) While waiting at the bus station, I came .... an old friend.
(i) When the business was sold, the family came .... quite a lot of money.

(j)   *The Barbados Advocate* comes .... every weekday.
(k)   Armed robbers planned a daring raid on a bank in San Fernando last week, but it did not quite come ....
(l)   I intend to give .... smoking from tomorrow.
(m) You should give .... to cars coming from the right.
(n)   The bridge gave .... under the pressure of the swollen river.
(o)   The former champion has now given .... his attempt to regain the title.

2.   For each of the sentences choose a suitable phrasal verb from the following list; if necessary use the past tense.

look up	make up	keep up	back up	pull up
draw up	speak up	follow up	check up	turn up

(a) The guests .... late for the party.
(b) It is a good plan to .... difficult words in the dictionary.
(c) I hope you will .... me .... when I put forward this argument.
(d) I can't hear you unless you ....
(e) I think these figures are wrong. Please ....
(f) I don't believe you. I think you .... the whole story.
(g) Superstars .... their run of wins by beating Paradise 1-0.
(h) You should .... your success in the General Proficiency exam by studying for the Advanced Level.
(i) We need some petrol. .... at the next service station.
(j) The selection committee .... a list of candidates for interview.

3.   For each sentence below choose the correct verb from those given in brackets:

(a) At what time do you think we ought to (walk/hurry/step/set) off tomorrow?
(b) The letters OPEC (make/stand/pass/count) for Organisation of Petroleum Exporting Countries.
(c) The plans for a new factory to be installed in Port Antonio have now (folded/blown/fallen/stopped) through.
(d) Pieces of the wreckage were (sent/poured/washed/brushed) up on the beach.
(e) The arrest of a senior civil servant in Georgetown has (sent/started/let/sparked) off a major political row.
(f) You should take out an insurance to (provide/establish/contend/deal) for your family in case of death.
(g) The firm's poor results (demonstrate/show/bear/prove) out what I was saying about the poor management.
(h) I should not like to (be/go/take/enter) on the responsibility of being chairman.

SOME DEVICES USED IN WRITING
Simile and Metaphor

The purpose of all speech and writing is communication. We can, however, vary our ways of communicating. Sometimes we must be strictly factual, as in a report, and use a plain, straightforward style to convey our message. At other times we may be telling a story and so we add imaginative touches and good descriptions. Perhaps we want to amuse the reader or listener. Perhaps we want to catch his attention or surprise him. When we add variety and interest in this way we often use *figures of speech*. These are striking, unusual and apt words or phrases which conjure up a picture or give a new twist to our meaning.

The two figures of speech that we are studying in this lesson are *simile* and *metaphor*. Both help to make language livelier. For example, we can imagine 'a very old man', but we have a more vivid picture of 'a man who is as old as the hills'.

SIMILE

This is a comparison introduced by the word *as* or *like*:

The ground was as flat *as a table top*.

Popular similes are often described as *clichés*, that is expressions which are over-used, such as:

strong as a horse	good as gold
black as night	quick as lightning
drink like a fish	mad as a hatter
bold as brass	dead as a dodo
obstinate as a mule	sober as a judge
light as air	white as a sheet
clean as a whistle	straight as an arrow
patient as Job	like taking candy from a child

A simile has two uses:

1. In exposition or explanation, it can be used to clarify a point:

    pressure We can liken the water pressure to six men who are pushing against a door and striving to open it, while the air pressure resembles six men pushing against the other side of the door to keep it closed.

2. In descriptive writing it gives a more vivid effect than the plain statement:

> The oak tree rose before me like a pillar of darkness. (Stevenson)

METAPHOR

Metaphor is also a comparison between two things or people, but it does not use the words *as* and *like:*

> He was a *tower* of strength.

It is possible to change this metaphor into a simile by saying:

> He was *like* a tower of strength.

Metaphorical language is used very frequently in everyday English, both in individual words and in common expressions. Here are some words used metaphorically:

> a *hollow* laugh
> a *piercing* cry
> *soaring* prices
> the *root* of the trouble
> an *iron* will
> a *concrete* suggestion
> a *corner-stone* of his policy

Here are some metaphorical expressions:

> to live from *hand to mouth*
> to be *out of one's depth*
> to *slap tar*
> to *get off the ground*
> to *bend over backwards*

Some metaphorical expressions relate to parts of the body:

> *foot* the bill
> make a clean *breast* of something
> to split *hairs*
> turn up one's *nose*
> lend an *ear* to
> have no *stomach* for
> to turn the other *cheek*
> be on one's last *legs*
> to keep your *chin* up
> drag one's *feet*
> stick one's *nose* into (someone's affairs)
> put one's *back* into

110

In written English, metaphors, like all other figures of speech, must be used sparingly and must be appropriate. Politicians who urge people to follow their advice are often guilty of producing what are known as 'mixed metaphors':

> The *ship of state is floating rudderless* and it's time we *put our hands to the plough* and *our shoulders to the wheel.*

In the above example there are three metaphors which are distinct in meaning and should not be used in the same sentence. The effect here is absurd.

EXERCISES

1. After each of the following sentences a list of possible interpretations of the metaphorical part of the sentence is given. Choose the interpretation you consider appropriate:

(a) The thief was caught *red-handed.*
     A His hands had red paint on them.
     B He was escaping.
     C He was in the act of committing the crime.
     D He was handing the goods to someone else.

(b) I am going to an evening class to *brush up my French.*
     A to learn French
     B to refresh my knowledge of French
     C to listen to a French speaker
     D to learn to speak French

(c) He was *carried away* by the music
     A lifted out during a concert
     B sent to sleep by the music
     C enchanted by the music
     D irritated by the music

(d) Errol is *out of his depth* in the mathematics class.
     A Errol is doing well in mathematics.
     B Errol is quite unable to do the mathematics in class.
     C Errol has finished all his mathematics.
     D Errol is trying hard at mathematics.

(e) Mr Samuel is *too long in the tooth* to deal with all these matters.
     A Mr Samuel is very old.
     B Mr Samuel has toothache.
     C Mr Samuel is very wise.
     D Mr Samuel is extremely busy.

(f) Some public servants are always *feathering their own nests*.
   A dressing up in smart clothes
   B decorating their homes
   C applying for other jobs
   D making money for themselves

(g) The question is — can Jamaica *ride the recession?*
   A Can Jamaica stay united?
   B Can Jamaica's government remain in power?
   C Can Jamaica survive a period of economic problems?
   D Can Jamaica remain at peace?

(h) Suddenly, one of the plane's engines *cut out*.
   A fell off
   B stopped
   C caught fire
   D made a terrible noise

2. Place the following metaphors in the appropriate spaces:

   long arm; root; teeth; seeds; ray; nutshell; circle; bare; foot; die hard

(a) one .... in the grave
(b) the .... facts of the case
(c) old customs ....
(d) the .... of the law
(e) in the .... of the gale
(f) the .... of the trouble
(g) the .... of doubt
(h) explaining facts in a ....
(i) a .... of hope
(j) a .... of friends

3. Match each of the words or phrases in Column A with one of those in Column B to form a suitable metaphorical expression:

A	B
climate of	savings
weight on	complaints
veil of	opinion
beat about	one's fingers
burn	secrecy
earmark	one's mind
flood of	the bush

112

MORE WORDS OFTEN CONFUSED

In Lesson 19 you studied pairs of words that are often confused because they are somewhat similar. Here is a further list. Look at the words, see how they are spelt and learn their definitions.

incursion	*movement into something*
excursion	*short pleasure trip*
torpid	*dull and slow*
tepid	*slightly warm*
inhibition	*a fear which stops you from doing something*
exhibition	*display*
contiguous	*near to*
contagious	*transmitted by touching (e.g., a disease)*
ingenious	*very clever*
ingenuous	*naive, innocent*
defer	*to put off/back*
deter	*to discourage*
access	*way to a place*
excess	*too much (of something)*
effusive	*too enthusiastic*
evasive	*trying to avoid*
intolerant	*refusing to listen to other people's views*
intolerable	*unbearable*
veracity	*truth*
voracity	*being greedy/having a hunger for*
personal	*referring to a person*
personnel	*staff/people employed by a company*
ensure	*to make sure*
insure	*to make an arrangement that secures a payment in case of accident, death or damage*
explicit	*clear/straightforward*
implicit	*not plainly stated but suggested*
stationary	*standing still*
stationery	*writing materials*
respectable	*proper/worthy of respect*
respectful	*showing respect*

innocent	*not guilty*
innocuous	*inoffensive/harmless*
formally	*according to rules*
formerly	*at an earlier time*
elicit	*to obtain* (information)
illicit	*against the law*
accept	*to take*
except	*not including*
emigrate	*to leave a country and settle in another*
immigrate	*to come into a country and settle in it*
device	*plan, scheme or small machine or apparatus*
devise	*to think up or invent*
prominent	*standing out*
permanent	*lasting for ever*
emotional	*full of emotion*
emotive	*likely to excite emotion*
impracticable	*incapable of being put into practice* (a plan)
unpractical	*not good at making things work* (a person)
militate	*go against*
mitigate	*alleviate/soften*
irrelevant	*having no connection with the subject*
irreverent	*not serious/disrespectful*
social	*living in groups*
sociable	*friendly/liking other people's company*
momentary	*short-lived/passing*
momentous	*very important*

EXERCISES

1. Write out the following sentences, using in each space a suitable word from the list above:

(a) We found the .... to the Roseau factory blocked by an overturned truck.

(b) The trouble is caused by .... of alcohol.

(c) He has an amazing .... for reading detective stories.

(d) .... and honesty are the two main characteristics I admire in a politician.

(e) Mr Hanna was .... elected deputy leader of the PLP at their convention.

(f) The newly appointed manager of the bank was .... a student of the University of the West Indies.

114

(g) The present schemes for using solar energy in Trinidad are quite ....

(h) The foreman on the building site was dismissed because he was too ....

(i) He had made an .... device for securing his car.

(j) His confession was quite simple and ....

(k) Read the question carefully and do not give an .... answer.

(l) Matters discussed at the Court of Appeal are rarely treated in an .... way.

(m) We received an .... welcome when we arrived at the reception.

(n) When questioned, the accused gave several .... answers.

(o) By winning her heat, Miss Gibson .... her place in the final of the 100 metres hurdles at the Stadium.

(p) I have .... my car from the 1st of October.

(q) The accused was declared .... of all the charges.

(r) The doctor said the medicine was quite ....

2. After each of these sentences, a list of possible interpretations of all or part of the sentence is given. Choose which you consider the right interpretation:

(a) There was an implicit warning in the chairman's speech that unless productivity improved, the factories would have to be closed.

The chairman

A hinted that unless the employees worked harder the works would close down.

B clearly said that because the employees were not working hard enough he was going to close the works.

C said that even though productivity had improved he had to close the works.

D said that he was not sure if the works would be closed because of poor productivity.

(b) The counsel for the accused pleaded that in spending the money he had stolen on gifts to his poor relatives and not using it for himself, the accused had mitigated his offence.

The counsel argued that

A he ought to be declared innocent because he did not really steal the money.

B the accused had confessed to stealing the money because he said he had spent it on his relatives.

C by spending the stolen money on his relatives he was not as guilty as if he had spent it on himself.

D the relatives were partly guilty in accepting gifts bought by the stolen money.

MORE FIGURES OF SPEECH

In Lesson 27 we learned about *similes* and *metaphors*. Besides these figures of speech there are others which help to improve our style in writing, giving it variety and sharpness.

IRONY

Irony is deliberately saying the opposite of what is meant, but in a way which lets the reader know the author's real meaning. The author Mabel Segun uses this device expertly in her book *Friends, Nigerians, Countrymen*. Here is a passage in which she gives advice to a provincial motorist driving for the first time in Lagos:

> First of all, he must break his driving mirror in pieces for it is not a necessary piece of equipment at all. And he must never look back before starting off because if he does he will not have the courage to move into thick traffic. Secondly, he must never signal his intention either with his hand or by using the car's indicators. This is a provincial habit and a despicable one too. And whatever else he does he must not stop at a road junction to make sure that the way is clear: people will think that he does not know his way, being a bush driver.

This is an amusing piece of writing, and more effective because it avoids saying directly what driving conditions are like.

ANTITHESIS

An idea is expressed vividly by placing it close to a contrasting idea:

> Speech is silver: silence is golden.
> Here today; gone tomorrow.

HYPERBOLE

This is the use of exaggeration, which we are not meant to believe, in order to create emphasis:

> When he was a baby, his mouth was so big his mother must have had to feed him with a shovel.

> I owe you a million apologies for my unpardonable error.

EUPHEMISM

Unpleasant subjects are described in pleasant terms. The ancient Greeks used this figure of speech when, instead of calling their wicked goddesses The Furies, they re-named them The Kindly Ones. The commonest euphemism is the contrived alternative for dying:

pass away   called to rest   pass to the great beyond

The *Encyclopaedia Britannica* says: 'Euphemisms are considered squeamish and affected by contemporary writers, unless used for humorous effect.'

EXERCISES

1. Identify these figures of speech:

(a) To err is human; to forgive divine.
(b) I have been rather under the weather.
(c) Thank you a thousand times for your kindness to me.
(d) Our dear mother went to her eternal rest a year ago.
(e) My holiday was an outstanding success. I spent the whole fort-
    night in bed with a dreadful cold!

2. Match each of the euphemisms on the left with one of the simple
    equivalents on the right:

terminological inexactitude	stupid
take industrial action	lavatory
senior citizen	a lie
the smallest room	go on strike
of low I.Q.	an old person
put to sleep	a fat woman
a light-fingered gentleman	kill
a lady of ample proportions	a pickpocket

3. Taking the example of the passage from Mabel Segun's advice
    to the provincial motorist, write a sentence in ironical style for
    each of the following:

(a) advice to someone trying to hitch a lift on a busy main road
(b) advice to someone going for an interview for a job
(c) advice to someone who is trapped in a lift
(d) congratulations to someone who has just won a big prize in a
    lottery
(e) warning someone against the dangers of slimming

LESSON 30

SYNONYMS

A *synonym* is a word which has very nearly the same meaning as some other word. Many pairs of words, which at first sight seem to have the same meaning, are slightly different. No two words are exactly alike; there is always some shade of difference in meaning. The following sentence illustrates the different shades of meaning of the words *remedy, cure* and *antidote*:

> One finds a *remedy* for trouble, a *cure* for disease, and an *antidote* for poison.

Although synonyms can be used as substitutes for other words, it is a mistake to think that synonyms are interchangeable. For example, the simple words *tall* and *high* may be regarded as synonyms. We may say:

> He is a *tall* man.

But it would be wrong to say:

> He is a *high* man

Synonyms are useful for avoiding monotony in writing, but this calls for judgement in choosing the right word. Look back at Lesson 3 and note the exercise in which you were asked to select the better word from pairs of synonyms.

If you are asked to choose a word *nearest in meaning* to a particular word in a sentence, you are expected to recognise a synonym. Read the whole sentence very carefully. It will help you to understand the exact sense of the word. Then you can more easily pick out another word of similar meaning. Here is an example:

> Her mother suggested she should buy more *durable* clothes.
> A comfortable
> B decorative
> C fashionable
> D expensive
> E lasting

The correct answer, of course, is *lasting*, which has a similar meaning to *durable*.

118

EXERCISES

1. Make pairs of synonyms by matching a word from the first list with a word from the second:

exterior	copy
duplicate	loathsome
connect	acknowledge
admit	outside
symptom	discontinue
cease	join
frigid	inducement
motive	indication
repulsive	cold

2. From the list of words or groups of words lettered A to E below each of the following sentences, choose the word or group of words that is *nearest* in meaning to the expression in italics as it is used in the sentence:

(a) The tax rebate was a *concession* given to the civil servants.
   A   prize   C   pension   E   payment
   B   reward   D   allowance

(b) The finance committee had *endorsed* the student's award.
   A   turned down   C   approved   E   increased
   B   reduced   D   refused

(c) Drug-taking should be *banned*.
   A   punished   C   allowed   E   encouraged
   B   prohibited   D   controlled

(d) He is a *prolific* writer. This year he has written three novels.
   A   clever   C   influential   E   very productive
   B   entertaining   D   well known

(e) The popularity of motor-cycle racing *waned* after five years.
   A   vanished   C   increased   E   changed
   B   declined   D   remained
                          unchanged

(f) The sports chairman said that Guyana might *boycott* the games.
   A   refuse to   C   support   E   advertise
       attend
   B   take part in   D   pay for

(g) The proposal was *obnoxious* to all right-thinking people.
   A   bellicose   C   offensive   E   tyrannical
   B   close   D   powerful

(h) All his attempts to revive the man were *futile*.

  A persistent   C clumsy   E skilful
  B successful   D fruitless

(i) Many journalists write about the Third World in *derogatory* terms.

  A appreciative   C disparaging   E patronising
  B mild   D critical

(j) The only effective *deterrent* which will put a stop to armed robbery is public flogging.

  A solution   C punishment   E discouragement
  B decision   D method

(k) Detection of tuberculosis is essential if the disease is to be *eradicated*.

  A wiped out   C caused   E diagnosed
  B cured   D understood

(l) We have to weigh the *options* that are open to us.

  A baskets   C rewards   E policies
  B choices   D burdens

(m) The new governor changed all the rules laid down by his *predecessor*.

  A opponent   C deputy   E legislature
  B the governor   D secretary
     before him

(n) Women outnumbered men at the meeting by a *ratio* of two to one.

  A count   C proportion   E increase
  B number   D total

(o) The dry ground *absorbed* every drop of rain that fell.

  A held   C flooded   E swamped
  B dried   D soaked up

(p) The doctor said it was not *ethical* for him to accept a reward.

  A lawful   C sensible   E respectable
  B morally right   D customary

(q) The Minister *advocated* a total ban on the import of whisky.

  A discouraged   C understood   E recommended
  B prevented   D agreed to

LESSON 31

ANTONYMS

An *antonym* is a word which has the opposite meaning from another. It must be the same part of speech. Some antonyms are different words, such as *solid* and *liquid*. Others, such as *loyal* and *disloyal* may be formed by adding a prefix.

If you are asked to choose a word which is *the opposite in meaning* to an underlined word in a sentence, you will be expected first to recognise the meaning of the underlined word. Here is an example:

Don't <u>offend</u> the gods of our fathers; it is not easy to .... .. them afterwards.

A admonish
B patronise
C control
D neutralise
E pacify

The correct answer, of course, is *pacify*.

EXERCISES

1. Make pairs of antonyms by matching a word from the first list with a word from the second:

majority	answer
bold	insufficient
convex	modern
negative	deteriorate
permanent	temporary
question	minority
shallow	concave
polite	timid
erected	increase
improve	rude
decrease	demolished
antiquated	positive
adequate	deep

2. Give the antonyms of the following by adding a prefix:
   (a) moral   (d) honour   (g) resolute   (j) audible
   (b) order   (e) sense   (h) truthful   (k) visible
   (c) perfect   (f) lawful   (i) proper   (l) important

3. By altering the suffix, give the antonyms of the following:
   (a) careful   (c) faithful   (e) powerful
   (b) faultless   (d) restless   (f) merciful

4. In each of the following sentences, there is one word underlined and one gap. From the list of words lettered A to E below, choose the word that is most nearly opposite in meaning to the underlined word and that will, at the same time, correctly fill the gap in the sentence:

(a) Mr Sanders is very generous but his wife is extremely ....
   A   talented   C   mean   E   moderate
   B   courteous   D   surly

(b) In his later years the famous soldier showed signs of senility; his vigorous .... had gone.
   A   strength   C   cleverness   E   wisdom
   B   youth   D   cunning

(c) There was a scarcity of mangoes in the market yesterday, but there seemed to be an .... of bananas.
   A   accumulation C   affluence   E   abundance
   B   effusion   D   increase

(d) Pride is certainly a less desirable quality than .... in a politician.
   A   envy   C   humility   E   courage
   B   honesty   D   tenderness

(e) Success or .... depends on the result of your examination.
   A   failure   C   elimination E   disappointment
   B   unhappiness   D   efficiency

(f) He was discharged with a warning after a former offence, but on a .... occasion he was fined heavily.
   A   next   C   further   E   subsequent
   B   similar   D   second

(g) Help for old and infirm people should be voluntary and not ....
   A   professional C   subsidised   E   supervised
   B   improvised   D   compulsory

(h) Joe's <u>kindness</u> towards his second wife contrasted openly with his .... towards his first wife.
A indifference   C cruelty   E arrogance
B insolence   D unfriendliness

(i) Parking on this side of the street is <u>permitted</u> but it is .... on the other side.
A stopped   C denied   E forfeited
B suspended   D prohibited

(j) While a good salary is a strong <u>incentive</u>, poor office conditions are an equally strong ....
A problem   C reason   E difficulty
B deterrent   D dilemma

(k) Africa is a continent of sharp contrasts in which <u>poverty</u> and .... exist side by side.
A fertility   C affluence   E magnificence
B benevolence   D plenty

(l) The school caters for some who are <u>partially</u> without sight and others who are .... blind.
A nearly   C almost   E usually
B totally   D mostly

(m) The judge was very <u>lenient</u> with the prisoner although the man deserved a .... sentence.
A brutal   C severe   E savage
B long   D heavy

(n) She was <u>seldom</u> seen at the market although her husband was ... there.
A usually   C at times   E often
B perpetually   D generally

(o) The house looked quite <u>dilapidated</u>, although the one next door had been .. ..
A renewed   C remedied   E restored
B renovated   D improved

SOME PITFALLS

Most errors in English arise from a lack of understanding of the parts of speech. There are some further special pitfalls which you should learn to avoid.

NEGATIVES

The words *not, no, nobody, nowhere, nothing* and *never* are negatives. Care should be taken to avoid using two of them in the same part of the sentence when only one negative is needed. This error is known as a 'double negative' and the following sentences illustrate it:

I *don't* know *nothing* about it. (*don't* = do *not*)
I *couldn't* see it *nowhere*. (*couldn't* = could *not*)

To be correct we must say:

I *don't* know *anything* about it.
I couldn't see it *anywhere*.

Sometimes a double negative can occur correctly when a negative adjective is deliberately used:

The result of the election was *not unexpected*

This is the same as saying:

The result of the election *was* expected.

Some words, such as *hardly, scarcely* and *seldom*, should be considered as negative words and therefore it is a mistake to use another negative with these words. The following sentences are incorrect:

We *haven't scarcely* any time left.
I *didn't* hear *hardly* anything at all.

The correct sentences are:

We *have scarcely* any time left.
I *heard hardly* anything at all.

KIND, SORT, CLASS and TYPE

We learned in Lesson 8 about the singular and plural of the demonstrative adjectives *this, that, these* and *those*. The singular form of the adjective should be used with a singular noun and the plural form with a plural noun. The following sentence is incorrect:

What do you think of these kind of people?

The mistake lies in thinking that the demonstrative adjective *these* should agree with the plural noun *people*. The noun which the adjective qualifies is *kind*, and therefore the demonstrative adjective should be singular — *this*. The correct form of the sentence is:

What do you think of this kind of people?

Similarly, we should be careful to say:

this/that class   this/that type   this/that sort (all singulars)

If, of course, the words *kind, class, sort* and *type* are themselves in the plural then the demonstrative adjectives will also be in the plural form:

These sorts of fruit are more perishable.

TAUTOLOGY (Redundancy)

This means saying the same thing twice in different words. Tautology can be seen in the following examples:

They came one after another in succession.

The words *in succession* mean the same as *one after another* and are unnecessary.

Gradually, little by little, Nelson increased his lead in the race.

Gradually means the same as *little by little* and either one or the other should be omitted.

Although the back seat was filled with luggage, but we managed to find room for another passenger.

Although and *but* should not both be used.

The first time, Parsons won by a knock-out in the fifth round, but, however, Marcelle got his revenge with a points victory at the second encounter.

The words *but* and *however* are doing the same job. Only one of them is needed.

Other examples of tautology include phrases such as:

repeat again (the prefix *re* means *again*, so *again* is unnecessary)
past history (history must be past, so *past* is unnecessary)
an essential necessity (a necessity is obviously essential, so *essential* should be omitted)

Students should note that redundancy tends to occur when dealing with abstract nouns e.g. His argument is not based on a valid foundation. In such a case, it is suggested that the sentence should be rephrased 'His argument is not valid'.

AS and LIKE

It is not possible to use *like* as a conjunction (see Lesson 16). The following sentence is incorrect:

This boy is behaving *like* the others did.

125

The correct word to use in place of *like* is *as*. In the same way, *like* is often wrongly used in place of *as if*. The following sentence is incorrect:

It looks *like* there is going to be trouble.

To be grammatically correct, say:

It looks *as if* there is going to be trouble.

Remember that *like* may be used.

(a) as a noun: I hope never to see the *like* of that again.
(b) as an adjective: We are of *like* minds.
(c) as a preposition: There it stood, *like* a giant totem.

Another point to note is that it is incorrect to say:

He speaks French *like* a Frenchman does.

The verb at the end of the sentence may be omitted and the sentence is then correct:

He speaks French *like* a Frenchman.

One particular colloquial use of *as* should be mentioned here. Although it is generally considered incorrect to say:

She is not *as* clever *as me*.

this form is accepted instead of the more pedantic

She is not as clever as I (am).

The word *as* is used

(a) 'for the purpose of, to do the work of':

You will be appointed *as* an accounts clerk.

(b) after *same*:

This cassette player is the *same as* the one I had before.

(c) in front of prepositions:

Traffic here, *as in* other big cities, is a problem.

(d) as......... as:

The young man cleared the weeds but *as soon as* they had gone, the bush took over.

(e) such as:

Agricultural crops *such as* cocoa remain an important section of the economy.

(f) as if:

It doesn't look *as if* it will rain today.

126

Mistakes often occur in the use of *as* for comparison. The following sentence is grammatically incorrect:

The Jaguar is as fast if not faster than the Mercedes.

A second *as* must be added after *fast*, to avoid mixing up two different constructions:

The Jaguar is *as* fast *as*, if not *faster than,* the Mercedes.

In all such comparisons remember to put in the second *as*:

She runs *as well as* if not better than Pat.

IT'S and ITS

It's is a shortened form of *it is*, the apostrophe denoting the omission of *i. Its* is the possessive form of *it*, meaning *belonging to it*:

It's likely to be a great fight.
The dog has hurt its foot.

UNCOUNTABLES

Uncountable nouns are those which have *only a singular form* and therefore cannot be used with *a, many* or a *few*. The following are some uncountables which sometimes cause trouble:

information   news   luggage   advice   furniture
weather   accommodation   knowledge   progress
scenery

MUCH, MANY, PLENTY, LESS, FEWER

These words denoting quantity sometimes present problems when used with nouns. You must first decide whether a noun is singular or plural.

Much is used with singular nouns:

I haven't *much patience* with Joe.
How *much money* have you got?
Has he *much influence* with the government?
There has been *much criticism* of her action.

Many is used with plural nouns:

Many aspects of the situation were considered.
His fame spread to *many countries*.
You have been warned *many times* not to do that.
The local traders offered *many goods* for sale.

Some nouns, however, such as *people*, can be treated as singular or plural, depending on the way they are used. If *people* is used to mean a group of persons it is plural, and you say *many people*, but there is also a sense in which *people* can be singular, meaning one race or nation.

Plenty is followed by *of* and the next word may be either singular or plural:

> Those boys have *plenty of determination.*
> Joe has *plenty of friends.*

Less means a smaller amount of, and it is mainly used with singular nouns:

> We are eating *less meat.*
> We have *less money* to spend this year.
> Please make *less noise.*

Fewer also means a smaller amount of, and it is mainly used with plural nouns:

> *Fewer men* are joining the army.
> There are *fewer jobs* for office workers

LIE and LAY

These two verbs often cause confusion. Here are some examples to illustrate the correct use of *lie* (which has the past tense *lay* and past participle *lain*):

> '*Lie* down on your bed until you feel better,' said Mother, so Patience *lay* down.
> When the fighting stopped the injured soldiers *lay* where they had fallen.
> She had *lain* for weeks, quite unable to move.
> The village *lies* at the foot of the mountain.

The verb *lie*, as you can see, is *intransitive*, that is, it takes no object.

The verb *lay* (which has the past tense and past participle *laid*) is, however, *transitive* and takes an object:

> The waitress *is laying* the tables for dinner.
> The police ordered the gunman to *lay* down his weapon.
> The bird *laid* three eggs in its nest.
> They had *laid* their plans carefully.

There is, of course, another verb *lie* (which has the past tense and past participle *lied*) meaning 'not to tell the truth', but this should not give rise to any problems.

EXERCISES

1. Make the following sentences negative *in two ways* by using the words suggested:

(a) For weeks he talked to everybody about the funeral. *nobody anybody*

128

(b) The petrol station is somewhere on this road. *nowhere anywhere*
(c) Joe scored some points for his team. *no any*
(d) Our dog will eat anything. *nothing not*
(e) He did something he ought not to have done. *anything nothing*

2. Choose the correct word from each pair in brackets:
(a) I have seldom seen (anything, nothing) better than this.
(b) She has hardly (any, some) friends (anywhere, nowhere).
(c) He has scarcely spoken to (anyone, no one) since that day.
(d) Seldom has (either neither) of the two brothers been seen in the village for the past year.
(e) Casuals have hardly (ever, never) won (any, some) championship cup.

3. Each of the following phrases is an example of tautology: Say which word in each case is unnecessary:

still continue	revert back	close proximity
final upshot	protrude out	sink down
new innovation		

4. Write out the following sentences with the word *as* or *like* to complete the gaps:
(a) Mr Grant's car is the same colour .... his brother's.
(b) This feels .... wool, but I don't think it is.
(c) George has got a job .... a sales assistant in Truvalu Stores.
(d) I remember the author .... a fellow student at U.W.I.
(e) Your pen is very .... mine.
(f) Daniel swims .... a fish.
(g) .... on many occasions, he has surprised us all.

5. Write out the following sentences, filling each space with the appropriate word — *plenty, much, many, less* or *fewer:*
(a) There are so .... cars going into the town every day.
(b) There was .... of rhythm in the music from the Melodian's Steel Orchestra.
(c) I eat as .... food as I can.
(d) As I couldn't sleep, I shouted at him to make .... row.
(e) The population of Barbados is .... than that of Jamaica.
(f) Although he has more relatives than I have, he has .... friends.
(g) We haven't .... time to spare.

COMMON MISTAKES

The lessons in this book have explained the correct use of all the parts of speech and the structure of a sentence. With this working knowledge you will be able to detect errors which are frequently made. The list of incorrect sentences given below is intended as a detection exercise. Be careful not to repeat the mistakes.

EXERCISE

Write out each sentence correctly:

1. Will you please do like I told you.
2. I shouldn't be surprised if they didn't go on strike today.
3. Which of us, you or me, do you think he likes best?
4. I sympathise for you in your misfortune.
5. This is the man who he tried to kill.
6. Those kind of people ought to be made to work.
7. I found your books laying on the table.
8. They are, each of them, experts in his own subject.
9. This is the student whom I consider will do well at the university.
10. Less candidates sat for the examination this year.
11. You can either take history or geography in the examination.
12. Neither Thomas or he wanted to come.
13. It was not his practise to drink alcohol.
14. The little girl spoke only when questioned by the teacher in a hoarse whisper.
15. *The Tribune* has a larger circulation than any paper in the Bahamas.
16. The old lady is never hardly seen nowadays.
17. Going out of control, I saw the car hit a wall.
18. The car skidded violently, so that it was the cause of the accident.
19. It is not economic to buy sugar in small quantities.
20. He is an engineer with two children earning $600 a week.
21. No sooner had we arrived but the rain stopped.
22. He had been waiting two hours until the bus came.
23. His self-assurance made him contemptible of the opposition.
24. The revolver was found by a security man in a brown paper bag.

25. People nowadays behave different from the way we behaved in the old days.
26. This is as good, or perhaps better than that.
27. He never has, and never will agree to your suggestion.
28. Trying to climb up the wall, the rope broke.
29. He was only there hardly an hour.
30. None of the boys were able to give the right answer.
31. A well trained dog always obeys it's master.
32. He said he hoped he will see me soon.
33. The two boys shared the mango between the two of them.
34. I decided I shall go immediately.
35. Everyone helped themselves to the food.
36. The climate seriously effected his health.
37. After exhausting enquiries, the missing person was found.
38. He was as clever or cleverer than his father.
39. This book has one page of it missing.
40. I gave him some good advices.
41. Mathematics are a useful subject to learn.
42. This medicine is very good in coughs.
43. The traffic is so dense that you can only now cross the road after a long wait.
44. Entering the room, the light went out.
45. The audience liked the song so much that we had to repeat it again.
46. Errol and myself went to the cinema.
47. I am ashamed for my untidy appearance.
48. The patient complained for feeling unwell.
49. This letter is addressed to both your wife and yourself.
50. He continues to remain in good health.
51. Please send a postal order, also a stamped addressed envelope.
52. Every girl must bring their gym shoes tomorrow morning.
53. The principle reason for not taking the job was the low pay.
54. Drink freely between meals of pure water.
55. The ship sunk in twenty minutes.
56. I am not one of those who believe everything I hear.
57. Neither Mr Richards nor Mr Martin were able to come.
58. The parcel was returned back to the sender.
59. I should have liked to have been there.
60. This is a matter for you and he.
61. Hundreds of cars went passed me before I was given a lift.
62. My house is different than yours.
63. The pupil with the least marks will have to take the exam again.
64. This camera is more inferior to the Japanese one.
65. Mr Davis, as well as Mr Gordon, were elected to the Board.

WORD-MAKING

Using your knowledge of the parts of speech learned in previous lessons, you can now enlarge your vocabulary. Starting from words you already know, you can find other related words. One noun may give rise to additional nouns, while nouns or adjectives may have corresponding verbs. Here are some examples:

Noun/noun	mission, missionary; custody, custodian; sale, salesman
Noun/verb	suspicion, suspect; reproof, reprove; portrait, portray
Noun/adjective	mischief, mischievous; talent, talented; shine, shiny
Adjective/verb	beautiful, beautify; strong, strengthen; long, lengthen

ROOTS

In Lesson 24 you read about prefixes and suffixes. Many of these came into English from other languages. Numerous English root words also arrived in this way. It is not, of course, necessary to know the original language in order to understand these words, but if you can recognise some of the common roots you will be greatly helped in your English language work. For example, did you know that words beginning with *audi-* mean something to do with hearing? You can think of a whole group of *audi-* words — *audible, audience, audit, audition, auditor*.

More roots derived from Latin are given in the list below, together with their meanings and examples of English words that have developed from them.

Nouns

aqua:	water	*aquatic*	navis:	ship	*naval*
manus:	hand	*manual*	miles:	soldier	*military*
donum:	gift	*donation*	urbs:	town	*urban*
populus:	people	*population*	annus:	year	*annual*
liber:	book	*library*	decor:	beauty	*decorate*

Adjectives

fortis:	strong	*fortify*	lenis:	gentle	*lenient*
primus:	first	*primary*	mollis:	soft	*emollient*
frigidus:	cold	*refrigerate*	durus:	hard	*durable*

Verbs

port(o)	carry	*portable*	voc(o)	call	*vocation*
dic(o)	say	*diction*	am(o)	love	*amiable*
scrib(o)	write	*inscribe*	ten(eo)	hold	*tenacious*
dorm(io)	sleep	*dormitory*	cred(o)	believe	*credible*

NEW WORDS

As knowledge grows, bringing with it new ideas, we need new words to express those ideas. Take, for example, the word *syndrome*. In certain illnesses doctors recognised a pattern of conditions which could not be described by the word *symptom*. What the doctors had noticed was a group of symptoms. The word that fitted this was *syndrome*. Afterwards this word was used for any characteristic pattern of behaviour.

Here are some words which are commonly in use today. They have all been made necessary by new ideas about science, economics, business, politics and government:

endemic	ecology	cycle	consensus	credibility
asset	category	dialogue	pre-empt	scale
transition	profile	strategy	bottleneck	stability

Of course, some of these words have been in use in the English language for many years. But they are now having to do more work. Take the example of a simple word *cycle*, which, as the following passage shows, is used in many different contexts:

> We can have a *cycle* of wave-motion, a temperature *cycle*, a song *cycle*, a *cycle* in ladies' fashion, *cycles* in the prices of stocks and shares, draught *cycles* and volcanic *cycles*. It is hardly surprising that the word occurs daily in our newspapers.

To satisfy the need for new words we have a number of compound words such as:

set-up	arrangement
goings-on	happenings, usually sensational
take-off	departure of a plane
let-down	disappointment
get-away	escape
climb-down	yielding, giving in
rake-off	illegal payment or profit
show-down	final argument to solve a crisis
breakdown	collapse
hold-up	armed attack or a delay
crack-down	firm action against something, someone
come-down	fall in importance or influence
write-off	complete loss

mix-up	confused situation
face-saving	preserving self-respect by appearing not to have lost
know-how	knowledge of how something is done

EXERCISES

1. Using the list of prefixes given in Lesson 24, try to match the words in the left hand column with the correct definitions in the right hand column:

collaborate	science dealing with triangles
reflect	someone of lower rank
transparent	to work together
monogamy	person who forces his way in
subordinate	to give wrong information
automaton	to send back light
trigonometry	(which) you can see through
interloper	marriage to one person at a time
misinform	machine that works by itself

2. Give the abstract nouns corresponding to each of the following:

(a) excite   (e) national   (i) parsimonious
(b) generous   (f) satisfy   (j) despot
(c) timid   (g) content   (k) simple
(d) mediocre   (h) philosopher   (l) inflate

3. Give adjectives (not ending in *ed* or *ing*) corresponding to the following nouns:

(a) access   (d) ecstasy   (g) rebel   (j) power
(b) barbarian   (e) ingenuity   (h) residue   (k) centre
(c) comparison   (f) marvel   (i) discern   (l) sobriety

4. Complete the following sentences, using the new compound words given in this lesson:

(a) After the accident, the car was a ....
(b) The government declared that there would be a .... on any sign of street violence.
(c) We must make every effort to develop our technical .... in order to exploit our natural resources.
(d) After being interviewed for the post and told that his chances were very good, it was quite a .... when he received a letter of rejection the next day.
(e) .... in marriage is often due to a failure to understand the other person's point of view.

134

══════ LESSON 35 ══════

MORE PHRASAL VERBS

Many phrasal verbs express a special aspect of a verb. Below is a group of phrasal verbs with the particle *off*. In this group the action of the verb with the particle *off* expresses 'completion'.

to bring off/to carry off/to pull off to succeed in doing:

Jockey Mullins pulled off a hat trick by winning three races at today's meeting at the Garrison Savannah.

to call off to cancel (meetings, arrangements, etc.):

The feather-weight title fight was called off because of the illness of one of the contestants.

to come off to happen to succeed:

It's a good scheme, but I don't think it will come off.

to cool off to become cool, to become less enthusiastic about:

Mr Miller's marriage was happy at first but his wife's feelings cooled off when she met another man she liked better.

to die off to die completely:

The flowers died off because of lack of water.

to doze off/to drop off to fall asleep:

I dozed off while listening to the sermon.

to fight off to repel:

The soldiers fought off the enemy attack.

to finish off to finish completely:

The century by Viv Richards finished off the chances of the Windward's team against Leeward.

to kill off to kill completely:

Disease has killed off many of the cattle in this district.

to leave off to stop doing something:

Continue reading where you left off yesterday.

to level off to make completely level:

I am levelling off this piece of ground to plant some vegetables.

to marry off to get rid of (daughters) by marrying:

Mothers like to marry off their daughters to rich businessmen.

to pay off to terminate employment with a final payment:

I've just been paid off. My job finished yesterday.

to sell off to sell completely:

The Departmental Stores are selling off all their men's suits at a reduced price.

to switch off to stop by turning a switch:

Switch off the television set, please.

to wipe off to get rid of (a debt):

After many years they managed to wipe off their debt to the bank.

to write off to reduce the stated value of something (machines, furnishing, cars, etc) to nil:

After the accident, the insurance company decided to write off my car.

Students should understand that many phrasal verbs are also idiomatic expressions and may not be acceptable in an examination paper. In a formal setting therefore it is more advisable to write 'quarrel' or 'disagree' rather than 'fall out'. It must also be noted that some phrasal verbs have more than one meaning e.g. 'Fall out' can also refer to military personnel leaving their formation.

VERBS plus two particles

Some phrasal verbs, as we saw in Lesson 26, consist of the base verb plus two particles, which together make a figurative or idiomatic meaning (given here in the right-hand column):

to come in for	to be heir to, to receive
to cut down on	to reduce
to make away with	to kill, destroy
to look down on	to hold in contempt
to be cut out for	to be suitable for
to live up to	to maintain or emulate
to do away with	to abolish, get rid of
to keep up with	not to fall behind
to give in to	to submit, agree
to fall back on	to resort to something
to fall out with	to quarrel with (someone)
to fall in with	to accept, agree with
to take up with	to become friends with
to run out of	to begin to lose
to run up against	to encounter
to gang up on	to form a group to oppose (someone)
to grow out of	to advance beyond
to be well up in	to have a good knowledge of
to work up to	to reach by stages

136

PHRASAL VERBS with OUT

break out	call out	carry out
make out	set out	sort out
wear out	wipe out	work out
go out	hold out	look out
speak out	stand out	turn out
spell out	let out	fall out

Look up the meanings of these phrasal verbs in a good dictionary.

POSITION OF A PRONOUN IN PHRASAL VERBS

When the object of a phrasal verb is a pronoun, it always comes before the particle:

He *wrote* the message *down*.
or
He *wrote down* the message.
He *wrote* it *down*.
I can't *make out* this word.
I can't *make* it *out*.

EXERCISES

1. Complete the following sentences with a suitable phrasal verb using the particle *off*:

(a) The Football Council of South Africa has .... a tour of the country by a party of British soccer players because of international pressure.

(b) My feelings for my son .... after he got into trouble with the police.

(c) I thought of a good scheme for deceiving the examiner, but it didn't quite ....

(d) I knew I was sickening for a bad cold, but I .... it .... with some strong medicine.

(e) I need only a thousand dollars to ...... the loan from the bank.

(f) The area where the explosion occurred was ....

(g) The Prime Minister's speech .... a furious controversy.

2. Use a phrasal verb with *two* particles to complete these sentences:

(a) You should ...... the amount of sugar you eat if you want to lose weight.

(b) Most women .... the problem of looking after the home when they try to seek employment.

(c) Joe wasn't .... a job in the bank. He was no good at figures.

(d) I had been away from school for three months and it took me some time to .... my studies in English and mathematics.

(e) The government would like to .... the employment of expatriates, but this is impracticable at present.

(f) The greatest danger for Trinidad is that the country may .... oil by the year 2000.

(g) Those with university degrees should not .... their colleagues who do not have degrees.

(h) The Minister pledged to .... the principle of unity and justice.

(i) The professor in the History Department has to be .... the history of the Caribbean islands.

(j) She .... me so much that I at last threw a plate at her.

(k) The other boy .... Daniel's plan to steal a car.

3. Choose a suitable phrasal verb from the list below to fill each of the gaps in the sentences. Put the verb in the past tense if necessary:

A make out   stand out   speak out   spell out   carry out
   turn out   work out

(a) The preacher .... against the wickedness of the people.

(b) The result .... to be a decisive victory for the Party.

(c) The tall building .... like a beacon.

(d) I .... a way of solving the problem.

(e) The doctor .... a thorough examination.

(f) I could not .... his handwriting.

(g) The increase in the price of oil .... a rise in the cost of foodstuffs.

B run through   see me through   pull through   get through
   sit through

(a) My father was so ill, the doctor said he would not ....

(b) I tried to ring you, but I could not ....

(c) Would you please .... the list once more.

(d) I am not going to .... that film again.

(e) I haven't enough money to ....

138

REVISION

1. Add *ant* or *ent* as required to the following:
   (a) intellig –   (d) differ –   (g) reluct –
   (b) brilli –   (e) attend –   (h) inhabit –
   (c) independ –   (f) relev –   (i) impertin –

2. For each of the following sentences choose the correct verb from those given in brackets:
   (a) He decided to (take/back/go) out of the scheme and withdraw his money.
   (b) After increasing for several months, investments have (levelled/straightened/come) off and now remain steady.
   (c) The officer (noted/checked/made) off the names of the soldiers from his list.
   (d) He (got/bought/took) out an insurance policy on his life.

3. Each of the following sentences contains a metaphor. A list of possible interpretations is given. Choose the one you consider appropriate:
   (a) I tried to be friendly with her, but she *gave me the cold shoulder*.
       A was angry with me
       B was not very friendly
       C pushed me by the shoulder
   (b) His friends said they were bored in his company because he was always *talking shop*.
       A talking about his employment
       B talking about things he had bought
       C talking about himself
   (c) The departure of the colonial power in Haiti *created a vacuum*.
       A reduced the population of Haiti
       B caused Haiti to be without a government
       C caused a shortage of food in Haiti

4. Make pairs of synonyms, using one word from each list:

voluble	aversion	still	loquacious
tranquil	stiff	rigid	prominent
fatigue	hermit	drunken	burst
salient	counterfeit	dislike	tiredness
explode	intoxicated	forged	recluse

5. Make pairs of antonyms, using one word from each list:

sour	frivolous	defective	obtuse
fail	perfect	serious	brusque
acute	irrational	reasonable	fiction
polite	hostility	complexity	succeed
fact	simplicity	friendliness	sweet

6. Choose the correct word from each pair in brackets:
(a) There is hardly (anything/nothing) grown on this island.
(b) I couldn't get a replacement battery (nowhere/anywhere).
(c) I haven't seen (either/neither) of these two films.

7. Choose one of the following words for each space in the sentence:

plenty much many less fewer like as

(a) This tastes .... butter, but I don't think it is.
(b) Poverty causes .... unhappiness.
(c) There was .... of noise inside the room.
(d) His nose is the same shape .... his mother's.
(e) Wages are very low and people have .... money in their pockets.
(f) If you travel before six o'clock you will find .... cars on the road because most people travel later.
(g) If you eat too .... sweets you will harm your teeth.

8. Correct the following sentences:
(a) Which of the two boxers do you think is the best?
(b) He never has, and never will drink beer.
(c) These kind of reptiles are only found in the desert.
(d) I do not wish to part from my watch.
(e) This is strictly between you and I.
(f) Checking through the figures the amount was clearly wrong.
(g) This is the man who she wanted to marry.

140

LESSON 36

TOPIC VOCABULARY
Finding The Words

In this lesson we shall begin to study words in the *contextual* sense. A test passage of 100 to 150 words contains numbered gaps which you are required to fill from a choice of five words for each gap.

Consider first of all what the examiner is trying to do. He is testing you on your understanding of the *whole* passage, not just on the meaning of individual words. The selection of the right word depends on how well you understand the passage. The theme of the passage may be specialised — it may be about banks, agriculture, education, Caribbean history, politics, business or some similar subject, so that some of the words will have a meaning related to the topic. For example, a passage about insurance might contain words like *premium, comprehensive, claim, obligation, mature, maintenance, deposit, policy, subscribed, transaction*.

The method of testing your understanding is called *multiple choice* because you must select the *right* word from a choice of several. You may think that more than one word will fit the gap, but only by thoroughly reading and understanding the whole passage will you be able to make the right choice from the five you are given.

First, then, read the whole passage quickly but carefully, without looking at the lists of words. Because the gaps will slow your reading, it is a good plan to substitute a made-up word like *tod*. This will prevent you from stopping to search for the right word until the second reading.

You will make your selection of the words on your second reading, which will be in short sections as you arrive at each gap in the passage. If you are not sure which word to select, try eliminating those which are clearly not suitable. This may reduce your task to choosing one of two words.

Remember also to pay attention to the rubric. This is as important as choosing the right words. It means *read the instructions*. It is surprising how many candidates in examinations fail because they have not obeyed the instructions on the examination sheet.

EXERCISES

For each question choose the word that is most suitable to fill the numbered gap in the passage. Record your answer as 1B, 2C, 4D, etc.

(a) The ....1.... of government was ....2.... from Spanish Town to Kingston in 1872, and from this date the growth of the city was ....3.... . Not even a severe ....4.... in 1907, which ....5.... many buildings, could slow its ....6.... into the twentieth century. ....7.... growth extended the boundaries of the city ....8.... and new harbour ....9.... have increased the commercial importance of the capital.

	A	B	C	D	E
1.	place	seat	house	assembly	power
2.	altered	taken	transferred	carried	transplanted
3.	evident	known	certain	forecast	assured
4.	disorder	landslide	riot	earthquake	epidemic
5.	ruined	spoiled	flooded	hit	demolished
6.	race	rise	expansion	extent	size
7.	suburban	outer	housing	building	estate
8.	edge	borders	extent	limits	area
9.	machines	aids	buildings	systems	facilities

(b) The contrast between the ....1.... green canefields and the blue Caribbean is pleasing indeed. In the evening the blazing sunset ....2.... everything with an extraordinary light. At night the Fedchem plant shines with its ....3.... of lights. Tortuga, a small village of about six square miles, is built on the most picturesque ....4.... point of the Monserrat hills. These hills must have ....5.... Spaniards with a name ....6.... of their own Monserrat of the Barcelona Province, with its jagged ridges, ...7.... the Latin 'mons serratus' which gives the idea of teeth.

	A	B	C	D	E
1.	fine	thick	lush	dense	rich
2.	shines	shows	burns	illumines	blinds
3.	clusters	myriads	groups	bunches	lots
4.	selected	suitable	important	vantage	desirable
5.	affected	inspired	told	struck	awakened
6.	similar	like	recalling	reminiscent	retrospective
7.	so	therefore	hence	as	how

(c) After the war, sugar and other agricultural production ....1.... the Barbadian economy, and for several years economic performance ....2.... the fortunes of agriculture. By 1970 the economy had achieved a measure of ....3.... , with sugar, tourism and manufacturing all prominent ....4.... of income, employment and foreign exchange. The ....5.... in sugar's importance has been striking, and results from the rapid growth of other ....6.... .

	A	B	C	D	E
1.	ruled	filled	dominated	led	affected
2.	told	reflected	achieved	acted	valued
3.	variation	equality	fragmentation	diversification	expanse
4.	sources	causes	means	ways	methods
5.	loss	decline	fluctuation	sink	decay
6.	crops	reasons	businesses	enterprises	sectors

(d) For ....1.... fees, insurance companies will help a firm insure against losses of all kinds and provide ....2.... if needed. Most firms will seek ....3.... against fire, theft, fraud and other ....4.... happenings for which they will pay annual ....5.... to the insurance companies. These payments will vary according to the ....6.... to be ....7.... Some of the happenings might include accidents such as ....8... at work or ....9.... debts.

	A	B	C	D	E
1.	fixed	graduated	suitable	appropriate	varying
2.	reward	compensation	payment	help	security
3.	aid	provision	protection	advice	prevention
4.	sudden	unknown	unpleasant	costly	unforeseen
5.	payments	sums	fees	premiums	costs
6.	risk	chance	danger	subject	item
7.	entered	undertaken	covered	agreed	included
8	harm	loss	damage	grievance	injury
9.	large	bad	illegal	overdue	unsecured

(e) On Good Friday 1979, La Soufrière suddenly exploded and sent a ....1... cloud of grey smoke ....2.... nearly five miles high, while cinders were ...3.... over a forty square mile area. One witness described it as being like an ...4.... blast, while another talked of a sound like ....5... thunder and a ball of orange fire. The forests on the crater slopes were reduced to blackened ...6... while the banana and coconut ...7... were covered in a ...8... of ash.

	A	B	C	D	E
1.	smooth	soft	mushroom	spiral	spherical
2.	racing	shooting	pouring	billowing	swelling
3.	showered	gushed	spread	rained	radiated
4.	piercing	organic	atomic	atmospheric	astronomic
5.	continuous	rolling	sudden	raging	blaring
6.	bits	stalks	stumps	logs	ashes
7.	farms	groves	gardens	plantations	beds
8.	veil	cloth	film	blanket	heap

(f) Players are ....1... by an armed guard as they enter and leave the field. In some countries police are ...2.... with tear gas. ...3.... of players are hanged when teams lose matches in Brazil. In England players are protected from becoming ....4.... for flying bottles by expensive fencing. Sport all over the world has been threatened by ....5... .

	A	B	C	D	E
1.	led	conducted	escorted	convoyed	surrounded
2.	supplied	prepared	equipped	geared	fitted
3.	figures	effigies	dummies	caricatures	models
4.	objects	victims	injured	targets	casualties
5.	bandits	hooligans	gangsters	vandals	savages

(g) Sportsmen, singers, actors and public speakers all ...1... the need to breathe from the diaphragm (the midriff) and not from the chest. In this way they use their full lung ...2... and have more ...3... over their breathing. They do not risk ...4... breath and they find diaphragm breathing a help in overcoming ...5... and anxiety. You cannot feel ...6... while you are breathing deeply at a slow steady ...7... .

	A	B	C	D	E
1.	know	feel	recognise	grasp	declare
2.	strength	power	content	capacity	volume
3.	control	direction	management	assistance	help
4.	losing out on	giving into	running out of	cutting down on	falling out of
5.	hesitation	illness	weakness	nervousness	faintness
6.	sick	inferior	speechless	discouraged	apprehensive
7.	speed	rhythm	pattern	rate	manner

(h) The word buccaneer is ...1... from the French term 'boucan', which in turn comes from the ...2... Arawak word. Buccaneers were sea-rovers who lived by ...3... . The little town of Port Royal in Jamaica came to serve as a ...4... for buccaneers intent on ...5... the Spanish and Dutch possessions in the Caribbean. The ...6... Henry Morgan was one of the most resourceful of the buccaneers.

	A	B	C	D	E
1.	come	proceeded	descended	derived	made
2.	previous	original	fresh	primeval	primary
3.	stealing	fighting	killing	piracy	trading
4.	base	town	home	refuge	fort
5.	taking	seizing	burning	raiding	robbing
6.	famous	evil	notorious	brave	terrifying

===== LESSON 37 =====

STRUCTURE TEST 1

The word *structure* is a convenient term to include all the grammatical ways in which we put words together to express meaning. In this lesson the exercise will, therefore, test you on the grammar you have learned in the previous lessons.

From the words or groups of words lettered A to D, choose the word or group of words that best completes the following sentences.

1. I saw my car .... from the car park.
    A was driven   C being driven
    B driving   D to be driven.

2. You are not eligible .... entry to the university until you have obtained the required grades in the examination.
    A of   C by
    B for   D to

3. You must share this book with your friend. There is .... book available.
    A not any   C no others
    B no other   D the other

4. The bank manager won't give me a loan .... I can provide a guarantee to repay it.
    A on condition   C unless
    B providing   D in case

5. I saw a 10 dollar note .... at my feet.
    A laying   C laid
    B lying   D lain

6. It is too expensive; we had better ....
    A not buying it   C not buy it
    B not bought it   D to not buy it

146

7. Oil is a (a) .... resource.

    A finishing   C infinite
    B finished   D finite

8. The principal gave me .... to help me with the choice of course.

    A a few advice   C some advices
    B some advice   D much of advice

9. I .... forget my cheque book when I go to the bank tomorrow.

    A don't need   C must not
    B ought not   D need not

10. He did apply for the job, ... ?

    A isn't it   C hadn't he
    B didn't he   D had he

11. The lesson has been .... till next Thursday.

    A put on   C put off
    B put over   D put down

12. I like both the Rover and the Renault, but I think the Mercedes is the ....

    A more reliable   C rather reliable
    B most reliable   D very reliable

13. The union leader urged his members to .... their rights.

    A stand up to   C stand to
    B stand for   D stand up for

14. I told him we were shut, but he pushed ....

    A in his way   C his way in
    B away   D his way

15. You don't need to pay if you ....

    A want to   C are not wanting to
    B want not to   D don't want to

16. People are .... nowadays than they were.

    A much less friendly   C more less friendly
    B much least friendly   D less friendly more

17. .... you start taking the medicine, the better you will feel.

    A Sooner than   C The sooner
    B When soon   D The soonest

18. I understood him .... he would come this afternoon.

    A saying   C he said
    B to say   D having said

19. He denied .... the money.

    A to take   C to have taken
    B to be taking   D taking

20. Journalists are usually .... about the news.

    A good-informed   C well-informed
    B well-inform   D well-informative

21. This exercise is .... difficult for a seven-year old child.

    A so   C rather
    B too   D quite

22. People expressed their .... by throwing stones.

    A resent   C resentments
    B resents   D resentment

23. I depend .... you to keep your word.

    A for   C in
    B on   D at

24. He does not express .... clearly in English.

    A his self   C oneself
    B him   D himself

25. I .... the bus at the terminus.

    A went off   C got out from
    B got off   D went from

26. You must .... on the form what subjects you will take in the examination.

    A regulate   C state
    B elaborate   D dictate

27. I've never spoken to her but I know her ....
    A from sight   C at sight
    B by sight   D on sight

28. They interviewed two girls .... the job was already filled.
    A in spite of   C unless
    B however   D although

29. His secretary .... the letters he dictated.
    A took on   C took down
    B took at   D took up

30. I would like you .... me with my English.
    A help   C for helping
    B to help   D to be helping

31. You .... not come if you feel unwell.
    A are better   C had better
    B better   D best

32. I know he is very ill, but I would like to get another doctor's
    ....
    A meaning   C opinion
    B advice   D interpretation

33. If you see anything suspicious, get .... with the police.
    A in touch   C talking
    B on   D through

34. He recommended .... the exercise three times a day.
    A to do   C doing
    B to be doing   D do

35. It would have been better for you to have refused the gift,
    .... difficult it might have seemed.
    A nevertheless   C in spite of
    B whatever   D however

36. The grass .... cutting yet.
    A need not be   C needs not
    B doesn't need   D is not needing

LESSON 38

IDIOM TEST

In Lesson 27 we learned how metaphor is used in common expressions such as 'to live from hand to mouth'. We call such expressions *idiom*, a word meaning that they are found only in a particular language — in this case English — and they cannot be translated word-for-word into another language. Idiomatic expressions are often informal and used in everyday speech. Here are some examples:

> The government must *bear in mind* the need for change.
> (remember)
> Old customs *die hard*.
> (struggle hard to stay alive)
> Why are you looking so *fed up*?
> (annoyed, displeased)
> We have now reached *the point of no return*.
> (from which it is impossible to go back)

We also learned in Lessons 26 and 35 that some phrasal verbs like *to do away with*, *to come in for* have an idiomatic meaning.

Only by extensive reading and listening to educated speakers can you become really familiar with such expressions. There are no formal rules to guide you.

After each of the following sentences a list of possible interpretations of all or part of the sentence is given. Choose which interpretation you consider appropriate for each sentence.

1. Mr Williams threw in his lot with the Party.
    This means that Mr Williams

    A opposed the Party.
    B gave all his money to the Party.
    C supported the Party.
    D threw something at members of the Party.
    E resigned from the Party.

2. The interval for refreshments took some heat out of the meeting between the union and the employers.

150

This means that

A the refreshments made the union and the employers feel cold.

B the union and the employers liked the refreshments.

C the union and the employers came to an agreement after the refreshments.

D the refreshments improved the relations between the union and the employers at the meeting.

E the union and the employers were very friendly during the interval.

3. The speaker was loudly criticised for his views, but he stuck to his guns.

This means that

A he did not change his views in spite of criticism.

B he remained silent after being criticised.

C he tried to explain his views when he was criticised.

D he was so angry at being criticised that he threatened his audience with a gun.

E he was so obstinate in his views that people criticised him.

4. Joe had his eye on the manager's job for a long time. This means that Joe.

A had been watching the manager.

B had been looking after the manager.

C had been chosen to take the manager's job.

D was afraid somebody else might get the manager's job.

E wanted to get the manager's job.

5. He went a bit too far when he took the headmaster's car and drove it round the school.

This means that

A he drove the headmaster's car too far.

B he ought not to have driven the headmaster's car.

C he found the headmaster's car a long way off before he drove it.

D the school was too far from the car.

E the car broke down when he drove it round the school.

6. What do you take me for?

This means

A What will you charge to take me?

B What sort of person do you think I am (a fool)?

C What work do you think I do?

D What nationality do you think I belong to?

E What are your thoughts about me?

7. If you take risks by buying cheap tyres for your car, you may, in the end, pay through the nose.

This means that

A you may be killed in an accident.
B the cheap tyres cost more than you thought.
C you may later have to pay a lot more — perhaps because of an accident.
D you may have to pay police fines for failing to have safe tyres.
E you may never finish paying.

8. Some people wouldn't put it beyond him to collect bribes from rival candidates.

This means that some people

A were not sure if he would accept bribes.
B put the matter of bribery entirely out of their minds.
C thought that only one side would bribe him.
D thought he would accept bribes from both sides.
E thought he would never accept any bribes.

9. The minister hit the nail on the head when he said that the biggest problem confronting Jamaica was low productivity.

This means that

A the minister's reference to low productivity offended a lot of people.
B the minister was exactly right in saying that the biggest problem was low productivity.
C the minister accused a lot of people of low productivity.
D the minister was exaggerating when he said that the biggest problem was low productivity.
E the minister made a mistake in saying that the biggest problem was low productivity.

10. The lawyer was obviously splitting hairs when he said that his client was not hitting the policemen, but pushing his hands against him.

This means the lawyer

A was making a useless distinction between hitting and pushing.
B was clearly in the right when he said his client was not hitting the policeman.
C was lying when he said that his client was merely pushing.
D was trying to deceive (a judge) by his remarks.
E was trying to be too clever.

152

11. The member accused the government of dragging its feet over the provision of better roads.

This means that the member

A said that the government was trying to prevent better roads from being built.

B said that the government was deliberately delaying the building of new roads.

C said that the government was unable to find the money to build new roads.

D said that the government could not make up its mind about building new roads.

E said that the government wanted to build new roads but people had to pay for them.

12. The student's murder triggered off a crisis in the university.

This means that

A trouble at the university ended in a student being murdered.

B the murder of the student ended the trouble at the university.

C there was a fierce argument at the university about the murder of the student.

D the murder of the student was the cause of serious trouble at the university.

E the student was murdered because he caused serious trouble.

13. Samuel doesn't see eye to eye with his brother over marriage.

This means that Samuel and his brother

A fully agree with each other on marriage.

B don't have strong views on marriage.

C hold strong views on marriage.

D hold different views on marriage.

E both agree that marriage is not important.

14. He will stick at nothing to gain power.
This means that he

A wants power but he is too lazy to work for it.

B will never do any work just to gain power.

C will work very hard to gain power.

D will never keep a job long enough to get power.

E is prepared to do anything (including something illegal) in order to get power.

STRUCTURE TEST 2

In Lesson 37 you were asked to choose words from a number of groups to complete sentences, to test your knowledge of various structures. In this lesson you are asked to choose an *interpretation*. This means that you have to try to understand not only the sentence, but also *all* the possible interpretations so that you can make the right choice.

After each of the following sentences, a list of possible interpretations of all or part of the sentence is given. Choose which interpretation you consider most appropriate for each sentence.

1. He must have forgotten to fill up with petrol.

   This means

   A It is not certain if he forgot to fill up with petrol.
   B He was obliged to forget about filling up with petrol.
   C It is very probable that he forgot to fill up with petrol.
   D He ought to have remembered to fill up with petrol.

2. If it wasn't for the expense, I'd buy a bigger car.

   This means

   A I want to buy a bigger car because it is more expensive.
   B I have decided not to buy a bigger car because it is too expensive.
   C I would buy a bigger car if I had more money.
   D I would like to buy a bigger car if it was not so expensive.

3. Every morning he would walk into the office looking extremely worried.

   This means

   A He wanted to walk into the office.
   B He always walked into the office.
   C He sometimes walked into the office.
   D He walked into the office deliberately.

154

4. The headmaster said she might just as well stay at school for another year.

   This means

   A She should stay at school because she had no other choice.
   B She might stay at school and do well.
   C Staying at school was probably the best thing for her to do.
   D She ought to stay at school in order to do well.

5. Don't spend more money than you can help.

   This means

   A Don't spend more than you have.
   B Don't spend money on helping others.
   C Don't spend more than you need to.
   D Don't spend money if you need help.

6. She was so beautiful she could easily pass for a film actress.

   This means

   A People would think she was a film actress.
   B She was mistaken for a particular film actress.
   C She was much better-looking than a film actress.
   D She was pretending to be a film actress.

7. I shall have to have my eyes tested soon.

   This means

   A I will give my eyes a test soon.
   B It will be necessary for someone to test my eyes soon.
   C I shall arrange for someone to test my eyes soon.
   D I shall soon have had my eyes tested.

8. We would have got lost if we hadn't taken a map.

   This means

   A We did not take a map and we got lost.
   B We took a map and we got lost.
   C We did not take a map and we did not get lost.
   D We took a map and did not get lost.

9. Unless you obey the intructions on the examination paper you will be disqualified.

   This means

   A If you do not do what you are told on the paper you will not be dismissed.

B If you do not do what you are told on the paper you will be dismissed.
C Do what you are told on the paper and you will be dismissed.
D If you obey the instructions you will pass the examination.

10. He may have seen his mother before he left home.

This means

A He had permission to see her.
B He did see her.
C He was able to see her but he didn't.
D He probably saw her. I don't know.

11. He had no sooner got into the bath than the telephone rang.

This means

A He didn't get into the bath because the telephone rang.
B The telephone rang just after he got into the bath.
C The telephone rang as he was getting into the bath.
D The telephone rang before he got into the bath.

12. They spoke so fast that we could not follow all they said.

This means

A They spoke very fast, but we still understood all they said.
B We followed all they said except when they spoke fast.
C Because they spoke very fast we were not able to understand all they said.
D When they spoke fast we understood nothing they said.

13. I didn't think it was an unreasonable suggestion.

This means

A I thought it was an unreasonable suggestion.
B I thought it was a reasonable suggestion.
C I didn't think the suggestion at all reasonable.
D I thought there was no reason for making the suggestion.

14. She didn't mind my mentioning her age.

This means

A She was not angry when I mentioned her age.
B She was angry when I mentioned her age.
C She told me not to mention her age.
D She forgot to mention her age to me.

156

STRUCTURE AND VOCABULARY TEST

In this final test, the sentences for completion contain a mixture of structures, that is, putting the right words together (grammar) and vocabulary items (lexis). Remember, once again, to pay close attention to the instructions.

From the words or groups of words lettered A to D, choose the word or group of words which best completes each of the following sentences.

1. The car stopped because he had run out .... petrol.

   A in   C for
   B of   D with

2. This novel is extremely poor; it ....

   A isn't worthy reading it.   C isn't worth reading
   B isn't worth to read   D doesn't worth reading it.

3. This is by .... the best picture he has painted.

   A far   C much
   B further   D even

4. The engine stopped ....

   A all sudden   C all of a sudden
   B all suddenly   D all with a sudden

5. Do you know what the .... is for calculating the area of a circle?

   A prescription   C formula
   B recipe   D model

6. He'll improve in time; it's only a .... of practice.

   A thought   C work
   B question   D need

7. I know that Dr Robinson said it was a hopeless case, but I think it would be wise to get a second ....
   A meaning
   B interpretation
   C advice
   D opinion

8. We have not arrived .... any decision on the matter.
   A by
   B on
   C with
   D at

9. His first .... to the news was one of total disbelief.
   A reaction
   B report
   C intention
   D sensation

10. I found this watch on the desk; I don't know .... it is.
    A what
    B to whom
    C whose
    D whose own

11. He must be deaf; .... he would have heard me shouting.
    A other than that
    B otherwise
    C although
    D rather

12. He was refused entry into the Air Force .... of his short sight.
    A in account
    B by account
    C for account
    D on account

13. She was able to give a .... account of the accident since she had been a witness to it.
    A first-class
    B first-hand
    C second-hand
    D foremost

14. I'm sorry; I sent it to the wrong address ....
    A by mistake
    B from mistake
    C with mistake
    D mistaking

15. Any citizens returning to Jamaica are required by .... to deposit foreign currency with a bank.
    A custom
    B law
    C authority
    D tradition

16. I left my pen at home; I'm sure this is ....

   A your's   C your
   B yours'   D yours

17. It was recommended that there should be another meeting;
.... , this did not take place.

   A in spite of   C because
   B instead of   D however

18. Students have been, and will continue .... on the campus.

   A to demonstrate   C to have demonstrated
   B demonstrating   D to be demonstrating

19. I told them I was not .... the phone.

   A on   C by
   B with   D for

20. Mr Bruce was elected vice-chairman but he would .... chosen
for the office of chairman.

   A rather had   C rather be having
   B rather have been   D have rather had been

21. You'd better wash your hands, ... ?

   A wouldn't you   C hadn't you
   B shouldn't you   D had you

22. My friend said he would pay me back .... when he could afford
it.

   A sometimes   C any times
   B some times   D some time

23. She has never got .... the shock of losing her husband.

   A at   C over
   B through   D off

24. It is .... to smuggle goods into Guyana.

   A illegitimate   C unjust
   B illegal   D improper

25. I don't like flying because I'm afraid ....

   A of crashing   C of a crash
   B to crash   D for crashing

26. At the back of Ali's Stores traders have .... the roads.

   A taken through   C taken on
   B taken over   D taken for

27. Dinah .... a white dress for her wedding.

   A choosed   C chose
   B choosing   D chosen

28. Mud and bamboo are .... building materials, especially in a climate noted for the violence of its rainstorms.

   A imperishable   C impotent
   B impermanent   D impregnable

29. She asked the bank manager for an overdraft but he ....

   A turned her over   C turned her down
   B turned it away   D turned against her

30. Don't hold on to it. Let it ....

   A go   C going
   B to go   D to be going

31. My car has just been cleaned. Therefore it .... cleaning again.

   A needn't be   C needn't
   B doesn't need   D hasn't need

32. He .... a complete recovery from his illness.

   A caused   C made
   B did   D had

33. He is .... to get very excited.

   A usual   C suitable
   B ready   D apt

34. He .... from smoking for six months.

   A abstained   C desisted
   B ceased   D rested